Arthur Willink

The World of the Unseen

An Essay on the Relation of higher Space to things eternal

Arthur Willink

The World of the Unseen
An Essay on the Relation of higher Space to things eternal

ISBN/EAN: 9783337159177

Printed in Europe, USA, Canada, Australia, Japan

Cover: Foto ©ninafisch / pixelio.de

More available books at **www.hansebooks.com**

THE
WORLD OF THE UNSEEN

AN ESSAY
ON THE RELATION OF HIGHER SPACE
TO THINGS ETERNAL

BY

ARTHUR WILLINK

London
MACMILLAN AND CO.
AND NEW YORK
1893

CONTENTS

		PAGE
1.	INTRODUCTORY	1
2.	THE PROPOSITION	11
3.	THE HIGHER SPACE, AN APOLOGY	13
4.	THE HIGHER SPACE	15
	(1) The impossibility of representation	16
	(2) Where is the Higher Space?	17
	(3) Not at an infinite distance	20
5.	LOWER SPACES	21
	(1) Space of One Direction	21
	(2) Space of Two Directions	21
	(3) Space of Three Directions	25
	(4) The mysterious nature of Space	32
6.	THE FOURTH DIRECTION	39
7.	THE WORLD OF THE UNSEEN	49
8.	CONCERNING THE DEPARTED	52
9.	CONCERNING THE VISION OF THE RISEN LORD	80
10.	THE APPEARANCE OF OUR SPACE TO THOSE IN HIGHER SPACE	90

		PAGE
11.	THE MINISTRY OF THE ANGELS	97
12.	SO FAR THE PROPOSITION HAS NOT PROVED UNREASONABLE	100
13.	CONCERNING THE OMNISCIENCE OF ALMIGHTY GOD	103
14.	YET HIGHER SPACES	106
15.	CONCERNING THE OMNIPOTENCE OF GOD	111
16.	DEFENDING THE USE OF GEOMETRY IN THESE SACRED CONNECTIONS	116
17.	OUR RELATION TO THE DWELLERS IN THE HIGHER SPACE	118
	(1) Our appearance	118
	(2) Celestial bodies	123
	(3) Bodies of Extension	133
18.	OUR HIGHER FACULTIES OR HIGHER SPACE SENSES	142
19.	CONCERNING THE KENOSIS, AND THE EARTH-LIFE OF OUR LORD	148
20.	CONCERNING THE RISEN BODY OF OUR LORD	162
21.	CONCERNING THE ASCENSION OF OUR LORD	165
22.	CONCERNING OUR OWN GROWTH IN GRACE	167
23.	SUMMARY	170
24.	A GENEALOGY OF THE THEORY	175

I

INTRODUCTORY

EVEN the most casual observer of the characteristics of contemporary thought must be struck by the appearance of many symptoms which speak of a prevailing restlessness in the minds of men.

Impatience of old boundaries, whether of creed or of opinion, is manifested by vehement denials of orthodox beliefs; and the same impatience shews itself in equally vehement assertions in favour of new standards whether of faith or morals.

Some persons, under the influence of this feverish restlessness, take refuge in a dreary scepticism; some in credulity or superstition. Some are led to exalt private judgement; some, submission to authority, as the only panacea for the cure of the uneasiness from which they suffer. Some, again, can see no remedy, and with however great reluctance, accept the conditions which they find so irksome, as being of necessity; and according to their dispositions, proceed as they would say, to make the best of what remains to them.

All, in whatever way, seek for some cure, or at least some alleviation of this epidemic; and no remedy can be suggested but has its troop of strong believers, no charlatan appears but finds a following.

In a word, the most opposite extremes of devotion and dissipation, of selfishness and self-denial, unite in this that they point to the existence of a deeply-rooted prevalence of dissatisfaction.

This restlessness, impatience, uneasiness, call it what you will, is not however all an evil. It gives a motive for a search after better things, and though in the search some individuals may go astray, the human family will eventually find a benefit.

Among the more hopeful aspects of the restlessness of which we speak is this, that it has driven men to look beyond this world, to think of the Unseen, whether of the future or of the present; and in it to seek for satisfaction, for freedom from the unrest of earth; in it to find some hope of peace, or at least of comparative repose.

A strong, even overwhelming desire is evident on many sides to gain some knowledge of the Hidden World and its conditions. Many Societies have been established on many different foundations, whose object, if they may be said to have a common object, is to investigate the phenomena of the Unseen.

The feeling that this object is of surpassing importance is very widely spread abroad; and the hold that it has taken on men's minds is clearly manifested by the enthusiasm of those who are dominated by it, and at the same time by the vigour with which it is denounced by those who oppose them.

It matters not what band of workers or investigators in this field of enquiry is selected, they will be found devoted to their self-imposed task; and at the same time there will be found in opposition to them antagonists who spare no effort of argument or ridicule to render their conclusions nugatory.

Both opposers and opposed, however much at issue among themselves, whatever theory they may uphold or condemn, agree in this, that the pursuit of knowledge of the Unseen is worthy of the greatest attention—the ones, since they engage in it so earnestly; the others, since they feel it worth while to combat the conclusions which have been arrived at.

Amid all their differences and divergences, they all bear united testimony to the hold which the Unseen has taken on the imagination of the day.

Chief among all associations, and far

above all societies of theorists however earnest, the Church of Christ is an undying witness to the attractions of the Unseen, and to the paramount importance of the study of the things which are hidden from our mortal eyes. She speaks of freedom, of liberty, of redemption from the elements of this earthly life, which is concerned with things visible and tangible; and points to the things which are not seen, contrasting them, the eternal, with the things which are seen, and only temporal. And her antagonists, her enemies from whatever side they marshal their forces against her, bear testimony, only the more strong in proportion to the strength of their hostility, in the same direction.

The forces of attraction and repulsion are opposite to one another, but the power is the same. One pole attracts, the other pole repels; but in both cases it is the power of the Unseen which is in action, and shews itself by its effects on all, however diverse those effects may be.

It is a very mysterious power. The whole subject is of course very full of mystery. But that is no reason why it should be avoided. Nor indeed is it a reason why we should despair of learning anything about it.

The term "mystery" is relative, not absolute. And though, from the Christian standpoint, the mystery of the Hidden World must be regarded as having to do with the most sacred subjects, still the strongest recognition of this sacredness does not carry with it a prohibition to investigation, but only a warning as to the manner of the investigation.

The spot on which we stand may be sacred holy ground; we are not on that account warned off from it, but only warned as to our behaviour while we stand upon it.

As a matter of fact there is nothing so sacred about a mystery as to forbid our trying to come to some understanding of it; there is no irreverence in endeavouring to penetrate into any of the secrets of Nature, however wide a meaning we may assign to the word Nature, even if we use it to include the GOD of Nature.

The Truth is sacred. Seeking for the Truth there is neither presumption nor irreverence, nor any intrusion into forbidden ground; always provided that the search is prosecuted in a right spirit; that is, with the intention of finding out the Truth, and not our own advantage.

Indeed, it is a matter of common knowledge that as time goes on many difficulties seem to solve themselves; many problems which appeared to be insuperably mysterious have worked themselves out into comprehension. It is as if the world, while sweeping onward in its course, were continually tearing apart the veil behind which so much is shrouded from our eyes; thus making it possible for those who are on the watch to see through the rifts something which before was hidden either wholly or in part.

In this way may be figured the gradual development of what has been dimly perceived before; as also the gradual perception of newer knowledge by those who look for it, or are prepared to recognise it when it is before their eyes.

Without for a moment forgetting or undervaluing the marvellous advances of scientific research in the physical world, or its results in revealing to us many secrets of Nature in its grandest as well as in its most delicate forms, it must be acknowledged that by many minds a still more absorbing interest is found in the thought of that which is not seen, and under our conditions cannot be seen by us.

This, the Unseen, is often called the super-natural or the supra-natural, but none the less it belongs to Nature, though in another and a larger and a higher development. And indeed we are not without grounds for supposing that, broadly speaking, there is a physical connection between that which is seen and that which is not seen.

Of course we must be prepared for an encounter with many difficulties in attempting to deal with what we cannot see. But after all, sight is not the only nor even the principal power which we possess; there are many other avenues beside that of vision through which we may approach a knowledge of the Truth.

This being so, that which is unseen is certainly not beyond the limits of legitimate investigation, and it may be hoped that it may be brought within the limits of a sound theory of understanding.

Of necessity any such theory must be at the first very largely tentative; and the evidence by which it is supported must be very largely circumstantial. " Proof in such a case can hardly be demonstrative, but it may be distinctly corroborative, and this too in a very high degree."

By many people, no doubt, any attempt to theorise about the Unseen will be condemned in advance as being purely speculative. But speculation, even in its wildest forms, has often led to very important and very valuable results in other fields of enquiry, and it may do the same in this case, if kept within due bounds of sober and rational restraint.

THE PROPOSITION

My object in this essay is to submit this as a proposition—"That it is in Higher Space that we are to look for the understanding of the Unseen," and to set forth some considerations which support the proposition, or at least seem to me to do so. And I would ask my readers to look upon the argument as a whole, suspending their judgement as it follows out its course, and regarding it as consisting of many threads, of which each alone is incapable of bearing the weight of the proposition, though together they have, as I hope, the strength which is necessary to support it.

It must be remembered that the only

evidence that can be produced is more or less indirect. But if it appears that the different threads, or the different considerations that will be adduced, agree with one another, and with the necessary conditions of the case, then they will lend and receive support, each to all, and all from each. And that which was doubtful will become more probable as repeated corroborations are brought forward, and from probability, I hope, it will advance to a reasonable acceptance.

III

THE HIGHER SPACE, AN APOLOGY

THERE can be but few persons who have not at least heard of the Higher Space, or, to use the more familiar expression, the Fourth Dimension of Space. It is a term which in some excites a good-natured ridicule; some hear it with a scarcely veiled derision; others treat it with a more or less respectful interest, as describing something very wonderful; some again meet it with the idea that it speaks of a purely mental and imaginary conception, useful it may be to mathematicians in their more abstruse calculations, as a means of solving difficult problems in the higher branches of their science; but I suppose that all or nearly all will agree in regarding any such application of the subject as I am contemplating, as being, if not fanciful, at all events very nearly approaching that position of affairs.

I think, however, that it may be shewn that the proposition is not fanciful, that this conception of Higher Space is not to be regarded as merely imaginary. On the contrary it is to be considered as giving us a hope of the greatest assistance towards the solution of questions in which we all have, or at least ought to have, a very direct and even overwhelming interest.

It would be highly unscientific to deny the possibility of the fulfilment of the hope which has been expressed, or to assert *a priori* that the Higher Space is and can only be the playground in which an ingenious imagination may disport itself unchecked. We will, therefore, endeavour to investigate this most fascinating subject, with some hope, however faint it may be, that as we proceed we may not impossibly discover something of value, or even of importance.

IV

THE HIGHER SPACE

As a preliminary it is necessary that the principles on which we shall have to depend should be enunciated with as much clearness as possible. And the result of various discussions has shewn that a very considerable amount of detail is not to be thought superfluous.

Without doubt even the most elementary idea of Higher Space is a difficult one to grasp; and although it is not really essential to my argument, still I cannot but feel that many persons would not be prepared to accept any conclusions unless that idea were set before them with some elaboration. It is quite sufficient if the existence of the Higher Space is taken for granted, and this assumption used as the basis of our argument, the principles being accepted till the deductions drawn from them have been examined. If these are consistent with each other and with what we know, either of our own knowledge or by Revelation, the preliminary assumption will be fully justified.

1. The first point on which we shall have to dwell is this, that there are very few indeed who can realise the idea of the Higher Space to the extent of picturing it mentally. Of these I am not one.

This power is no doubt a very enviable one; but though it be lacking, the want of it does not in the least degree interfere with the acceptance of the proposition before us. It will amply suffice, as has been said, if the principles are grasped, and the argument will not suffer in any way so long as this is the case.

We start then from this point, that we cannot illustrate the conception of the

Higher Space even in the most diagrammatic way upon a blackboard. It is at first a purely mental conception, and the only way in which it can be approached is by degrees.

2. At the very outset we are met by a difficulty, which expresses itself in the question, Where is there any room for this Higher Space?

Our natural ideas of our own Space, based upon our personal experience, lead us to imagine, among other things, that it extends on all sides of us. Thus, when we try to think of other Worlds or other Spaces, we are inclined to think of them as if they were at a very great distance from us.

That is to say that we think of our World or our Space, as if it were in the centre of the Universe, occupying a vast sphere, while beyond that sphere there may be other Worlds or Systems or Spaces, occupying still vaster spherical envelopes.

Or it may be that we think more humbly of our Space, and, with a greater modesty, regard it as being in some obscure corner of the Universe, forming a block, so to speak, of Space, beyond which other blocks of some kind or other exist, and represent other Worlds or Systems or Spaces.

Or again, it may be that these expressions only represent to our minds something connected with the stars and planets and constellations. This last view is only mentioned for the purpose of pointing out that all these bodies are situated in our Space, so that no reference to them is possible when the expression, "Other Worlds," is used. Higher Space is outside our Space, and it is therefore outside our Space that room is to be found for it. Distance does not enter into the question at all; it is only with Direction that we have to do.

This is the first of all the principles which we have to get hold of; it is a fact which must be borne in mind; else there is no hope of understanding the subject at all.

We will try to make this quite clear. It may be seen in this way. Astronomers have taught us that our Space is practically illimitable. Figures are lost in the depths of Space. Thousands of miles are as unconsidered trifles in the computation of the distances of even the nearest stars. And far away beyond them our Space still extends indefinitely, till the mind is staggered in the endeavour to appreciate, however inadequately, the extent of our own Space.

The only escape that we can find from hopeless despair in the attempt to describe the distance of the boundary of our Space, is to say that it is infinite. This really means that we do not know anything about it, that we cannot fix a limit beyond which our Space does not extend.

This being so, the pertinence of the enquiry, Where is there any room for Higher Space? is to be seen. If such a

Space does exist outside our Space, does it lie beyond the infinitely distant boundary? Or where?

3. If the foregoing were the only idea of Space with which we are acquainted, it would, indeed, be hopeless to attempt to realise anything belonging to other Worlds or Spaces. Remove them to as great a distance as you will, they are still not removed beyond that infinitely distant boundary of our own Space. In other words there is no room in that direction for a Higher Space.

V

LOWER SPACES

1. But this is not our only idea of Space. We can and do speak of inferior Spaces. By thinking of them our minds may be prepared for the recognition of the existence of Higher Space, existing not at a distance such as no figures can express, but elsewhere, in some new direction with which we are not practically acquainted. This, as I have said, by degrees.

2. The first of these steps is to be taken by confining our thoughts to a single straight line, resolutely excluding from our minds anything and everything outside that one straight line.

Suppose that this is done. Now we are

thinking of Space of One Dimension, or, as we may call it, of One Direction; since under these conditions motion can only take place along that line. That is, if a point is travelling under these conditions, it can only trace or retrace that line. Backwards or forwards it is the same line along which it moves and no other. Only one direction is possible, that is along the one straight line, outside of which it cannot be transported.

This is the simplest and most elementary idea of Space that can be put before our minds. In other words it is the Lowest Space of which we can think.

Though speaking of it as a straight line, it is not to be regarded as a mathematical straight line, for that consists of length without breadth, and is imaginary, not physical. We are thinking of physical Space, it must therefore be regarded as being wide enough for an atom to move along it.

To make the conception of this Lowest

Space as clear as possible, we will represent it by a straight tube of glass of the smallest conceivable section, perfectly smooth inside, and just large enough for the smallest possible subdivision of matter to pass along it. The bore of the tube is Space of One Direction. It is of indefinite tenuity, but it is thinkable.

I dwell on this because it is important that from the first our minds should familiarise themselves with the thought of the limitations of Low Space. And because we can examine the conditions of this Lowest Space with accuracy.

Since the diameter of the tube is the smallest possible, it is evident that any being in this Space must fill up the tube entirely from side to side. He may be of any length, but he cannot be thicker than the tube. This means that he cannot pass another being in that Space.

Childish as this observation may seem to be, it is not without its importance ; for it makes it evident that the possibilities of existence, whether physical or mental, are terribly restricted in the Lowest Space. Activity of either kind is forbidden, according to our notions. There is very little to do, and very very little to think about.

Still, though this Space is so extremely limited, it is impossible to know all about it.

Supposing that one single being dwelt in it, he could travel for ever either backwards or forwards to an infinite distance. He could only be really acquainted with the monotonous condition of his momentary resting-place.

And even we, regarding his Space from outside, through the transparent walls of it, cannot know all about it; for beyond the small extent in our immediate neighbourhood, we can only depend upon the principles of Analogy and Continuity in our speculations as to the conditions prevailing at different points of the Space.

Even here on the threshold of our investigations of Space the Mystery of

Space confronts us. There is no escape from it.

For even in this most restricted conception of Space, the very lowest which we can call physical, we are met by the idea of infinity, which bids us beware of supposing that even such an apparently simple idea as that of one straight line is to be completely grasped by our powers of thought. Our knowledge cannot be complete even in respect of Space of One Direction; it is only close to us that we can absolutely know what is going on. Beyond that, deduction and inference and reasoning lead us, and we are content to follow their guidance, but without them we should be in hopeless ignorance of all beyond our reach.

3. We will now take another step, and, rising a little in the thought of Space, turn our minds to what exists at the two sides of our straight line.

This is a Plane or Surface. Not, indeed, a mathematical plane which possesses only the properties of length and breadth; that is an imaginary conception, ours is physical.

We may represent this Space as we did the Lower Space, by thinking of two perfectly smooth flat plates of glass, lying parallel to each other, and so close to each other that they are separated only by the thickness of an atom.

Giving our minds liberty to act in this Space, but not above or below it, we find that we are able to think of motion, not only in a backwards and forwards direction, but also to the right and left.

A new Direction has been introduced. This Space is known as Space of Two Dimensions, or, as we may call it, of Two Directions, since in addition to the One Direction that we found along the straight line, we may now diverge to either side of it.

It is convenient to think of these divergences as taking place to the right or left along lines at right angles to the original straight line, because in this way there is the least confusion introduced into the discussion of motion in this Space.

We will, therefore, consider a point moving in Space of Two Directions in this way. Or rather, to import a little human interest into the consideration, we will suppose that we are watching some being through the plate of glass above him.

In order that the idea may be as vivid as possible, we will think of him as if he were like one of those shadow pictures which we sometimes see on the walls of old houses. What we shall see is this. He can travel from any one point to any other, by going first for a certain distance along one straight line, and then by going for a certain distance along another straight line at right angles to it. As a rule he will go straight from one position to the other. But this is only because he likes to take a short cut; we know that he can make his journey in the way which we have mentioned.

When, therefore, we wish to describe the Space in which he moves, in the simplest way, we say that by a judicious use of Two Directions only, he can get from any one place to any other.

When we look a little closer, we see that this being fills up the whole of his Space from side to side. If therefore he wishes to pass another being in his Space he can only do it by jumping or climbing over his head, or crawling under his feet. He cannot turn round, he can only see what is before him. And of course he cannot see anything which lies outside the plates which enclose him. His senses are only adapted for the Space in which he dwells, he cannot by means of any of them perceive anything outside of it.

But at the same time we observe that he is infinitely better off than a being in the Lower Space of only One Direction, he is not compelled to confine himself to the utterly monotonous existence in the tube, his ideas are of a higher order than those of the lower being; compared to them his powers are of an infinitely extended nature, he can think of what the lower being could not conceive, he is in the enjoyment of a Greater Freedom, although to our notions even that is sadly limited.

Although this Space is to our perceptions very limited, still as before it is not possible to know all about it. There is no limit beyond which we can say that farther motion is impossible. Our friend may take his journey with an acquaintance behind him, and travel to any distance, and then it will always be possible to think of going farther. He can never be said to know the conditions of any part of his Space which he has not visited. And even we who can look down upon his Space, and see through the plate of glass what is going on in it, cannot know all about that Space; for beyond the small extent of it in our own immediate neighbourhood, we can only depend upon the principles of Analogy and Continuity in our speculations as to the conditions prevailing at different points of the Space.

The idea of infinity comes in, to warn us of the existence of the Mystery of Space, and to remind us that what we know outside the very narrow limits of our own observation, we can know only by a process of reasoning or deduction or inference, although we are content to consider them as being trustworthy guides.

There are two observations to be made in this place which are of great importance to the developing of our future argument. This is the first. That we perceive that an infinite number of tubes such as represented the Lowest Space may be laid side by side in the Space of Two Directions, this means that the Space of Two Directions is of an infinitely greater extent than the Space of one Direction. That is that the infinity of the Lower Space is swallowed up in the infinity of the Higher; so that this latter though it includes the former may be regarded as practically independent of it. So small a portion of it is occupied by the comparatively insignificant tube, that from the lower point of view, the whole of the Higher Space may be regarded as lying outside the Inferior Space, and beyond it. At the same time the Higher Space is in absolute contact with every point of the Lower Space, at the two sides at the Right and Left. Not at an infinite distance from it.

Already then there appears a faint glimmering of the answer to the question, Where is there any room for the Higher Space?

The second observation is this. In passing from the Lower Space of One Direction to the next Higher Space of Two Directions there is an enormous increase in the power of the mind, proportional to the increase of the Space in which it works. At once it becomes emancipated from the very narrow limits imposed upon it while it was confined in its operations to Space of One Direction, and it revels in the sense of comparatively very much Greater Freedom.

4. We are now ready to take another step. We will introduce the idea of a Third Direction, that is we will no longer confine ourselves to the plane Space shut in between the two glass plates; but, removing them, permit ourselves to rise above or sink below it. This brings in the conception of thickness, or of what we call solid things.

Up to the present we have only been able to think of flat things. Everything has been perfectly flat, possessing only length and breadth, with the minimum of thickness which is required for any physical perception of them at all. Now beside length and breadth things may have the property of thickness.

This Space to which we have come is known as Space of Three Dimensions, or in the same way as before we may call it Space of Three Directions; for now we are able to think of motion as being possible and taking place—

(i.) Backwards or Forwards. (ii.) To the Right or Left. (iii.) Up or Down.

In the same way as before we notice that by a judicious use of motion in these three directions we can reach any one point in this Space from any other point. That is by moving for a certain distance along one straight line, then for a certain distance along another straight line at right angles to it, and then along another straight line at right angles to the plane in which the two former lines were drawn.

Of course there is a nearer way of making the journey; but since every journey may be analysed in this manner, it is evident that only the three directions of which we are speaking are necessary, and therefore that the name which has been given to this Space is a true description of it.

At the risk of being tedious I must repeat the observations which have already been made as to the relations of the two Lower Spaces; for it is desirable to familiarise the mind with the principles which they involve.

First, then, the Higher Space of Three Directions is of infinitely greater extent than the Lower Space of Two Directions. Or, to put it in the clearest way, there is room in it for an infinite number of Spaces of Two Directions piled one upon another. The infinity of the Lower Space is swallowed up in the higher infinity of the Higher Space, so that this latter is practically independent of the former, and may be considered as lying outside of it, and beyond it; while at the same time the Higher Space is in perfect contact with every point of the Lower Space through its whole extent, not at an infinite distance from it.

Secondly, in passing from the Space of Two Directions into the Higher Space of Three Directions, there is an enormous increase in the power of the mind, proportional to the increase of the extent of the Space in which it works. It has become emancipated from the very narrow limits of the flat Space, and rejoices in the sense of a higher liberty and a Greater Freedom.

I will just set down in passing, though it may hardly be necessary, that this Space of Three Directions is the Space in which we live.

So far we have been considering what is before our eyes, and by using almost identical expressions, we have found our way from Space of One Dimension or One Direction through Space of Two Dimensions or Two Directions, to Space of Three Dimensions or Directions. The same kind of process has been followed with exactness.

On the way we have seen that the Higher Space of Two Directions is in perfect contact with Space of One Direction; though to an intelligent being in the Lower Space it would naturally be conceived as being at an infinite distance, since it lies beyond his range. And in the same way we have seen that Space of Three Directions is in perfect contact with Space of Two Directions, though to an intelligent being in the Lower Space it would naturally be conceived as lying at an infinite distance, since it is beyond his range.

These results must be borne in mind.

In view of the next step which we are about to take, this farther observation is desirable, viz. That we must recognise the existence of the mystery of Space here in the Space with which we are most familiar, as well as in the Inferior Spaces with which we have been occupying ourselves up to the present. Beyond the very narrow range of our own personal experience, we have to depend very largely on the principles of Analogy and Continuity for our ideas of what goes on in the depths of Space. We cannot see beyond a very little way into the farther distances of Space. And even when our vision is reinforced by the telescope, the additional penetration of Space which is within our power is comparatively small when we consider the infinite depths of it. And yet we are quite content to draw our conclusions by reasoning from what we see as to the conditions of what we cannot see, or at best can only very dimly perceive.

And more than this, since, as we have said, we are not concerned with distances so much as direction, it is well that we should recognise the fact that our ideas of direction are by no means to be depended on. With us direction is relative, not absolute. Let it be supposed that there are two men standing at the two poles of the Earth, and two more on the Equator, these two latter looking towards each other, that is one looking East and the other looking West. Now when the man at the North Pole points Up, the man at the South Pole says that the direction is not Up but Down; while the two at the Equator are not only at issue with them, but also at the same time at issue between themselves. The direction in which the first is pointing is to the one looking East neither Up nor Down, but to the Left; while to his brother who is looking West it is as certainly to the Right. From this we see that our ideas of direction are not by any means absolute, but purely personal, or at the best conventional.

VI

THE FOURTH DIRECTION

In passing from the thought of Space of Three Dimensions or Directions to Space of Four Directions, we shall have to introduce a new direction. But though at first this may appear to be a difficulty, if the result of the little illustration above has been taken to heart, it will not be at all insuperable.

As before, all that we have to do is to give our minds liberty to imagine another Direction beside the three with which we have been engaged. If our minds have been confused by the thought of the mystery of Space as we have seen it in the Inferior Spaces as well as in our own, and by the bewildering differences in the estimation of directions among ourselves from which we can only escape by the use of conventional expressions, no new effort will be called for, a repetition of the one which we have already made will be sufficient. And it may be repeated once more that a clear comprehension of the new direction is not by any means essential to the developing of the proposition before us. Indeed, if we had to wait till this new direction should be realised, we should have to wait a very long time, and then probably be disappointed.

With the introduction of the new Direction we must give it a name. The only name that can be given is something like this, The Fourth Direction. For this Direction being one with which we are not acquainted, we cannot give it any descriptive name, and it is therefore desirable to make use of a name which shall not commit us to anything beyond our experience, and which at the same time does not open out the possibility of any misapprehension.

Now we are to think of motion as being more complicated in analysis than before, though at the same time more free; since we conceive of it as taking place in a new direction as well as those with which we are acquainted. Of course this new direction is not only along the line of the Fourth Direction which is at right angles to the three mutually perpendicular lines of which we have experience [though that line is taken as being typical of the Space, in the same way as the Up and Down line was taken as being typical of the Space of Three Directions in comparison with the Space of Two Directions; and the Right and Left line, of the Space of Two Directions in comparison with the Space of One Direction], there are an infinite number of directions compounded between each one of the Three and the new Fourth Direction. That is, we are no more compelled to confine our energies to three directions only, since a Fourth Direction with its infinite number of combinations is opened to us so that our range is extended indefinitely.

Of course I am only speaking of our mental range, for in our present conditions this Higher Space is altogether beyond our physical reach.

Making use of almost the same phraseology as before, we recognise the fact that this Higher Space of Four Directions is of infinitely greater extent than the Lower Space of Three Directions. The infinity of our Space is swallowed up in the higher infinity of the Higher Space, so that the latter is practically independent of the former, and may be regarded as lying outside it and beyond it, while yet it is in perfect contact with every point of our Space in its whole extent. Not at an infinite distance from it.

And moreover the same observation may be made as in the earlier cases, viz. that an infinite number of Spaces such as ours may be accumulated one on another, within the limits of the Higher Space of Four Directions.

This is a terribly hard thing to realise in any way, but it is evidently a fact, and to accept it is a help in recognising some of the conditions of the Higher Space.

We have now found the answer to the question, Where is there any room for a Higher Space? It lies in the Fourth Direction.

Step by step, using almost the same words, we have risen from the conception of Space of One Direction to that of Space of Four Directions. The process has been identically the same. The principles of Analogy and Continuity, to which we looked for guidance in the farther regions of the Lower Spaces, as well as in the distances of our own Space, the only principles on which we could depend for knowledge of anything beyond our immediate neighbourhood, have been found to be available in this case also. So that now we see our way to some understanding of the Higher Space of Four Directions, at least so far as this, that there is a logical ground for the acceptance of the conception of it as existing—Somewhere.

The fact that we cannot point in the Fourth Direction need not trouble us. This is not to be expected. For as we have seen in considering the Inferior Spaces, even intelligent beings in a Lower Space are utterly unable to recognise the Direction which is characteristic of the next Higher Space, so much so that they naturally think of it as lying at an infinite distance, while yet to our perceptions it is absolutely near to them.

In the same way to our natural ideas concerning it, the Higher Space of Four Directions seems to be at an infinite distance, simply because it lies in an unknown direction, of which we cannot be cognisant. And the Unknown is naturally relegated to a great distance.

There are, as I have said, some favoured

individuals who can see in their mind's eye the line which is drawn in the Fourth Direction. Though there are but a few of them, the rest of us may find a satisfaction in knowing that this Direction can be mentally pictured by some gifted persons; and those who have had their doubts about its real existence, may in some degree be reassured by the knowledge that it is real to some, although that experience is not shared by all.

But after all we do not depend only upon this fact, nor on the analogy which the pursuit of our argument has set before us.

The foregoing has only been an attempt at a translation into ordinary language of what mathematicians have taught us. They are easily able to shew far more than a possibility of the existence of this Fourth Direction.

They can write down expressions which seem to represent figures in Space of Four Directions, and then make sections of them which we can at once recognise as being real, not fanciful.

Thus for example—

$$x^2 + y^2 + z^2 + w^2 = r^2$$

represents a figure in Space of Four Dimensions.

The Section of it in our own Space is—

$$x^2 + y^2 + z^2 = r^2$$

which is a Sphere, of which the radius is r.

The operation is exactly the same as that by which we find the Section of the Sphere in Space of Two Dimensions, which is—

$$x^2 + y^2 = r^2,$$

and represents a circle, of which the radius is r.

This brings the Fourth Direction of Space into the region of real existences. For it is far harder to imagine that there can be real sections of things which do not exist, than to believe in the existence of real figures when we see the sections.

Of course in endeavouring to translate the accounts of operations in the Higher Geometry into plain English, the exceedingly idiomatic language of the original has made it impossible to represent it satisfactorily. Much therefore has been lost. But, however, enough has been preserved to introduce the idea of Higher Space, and to make the meaning of the term to some extent intelligible. Sufficiently so, I trust, for its adoption as the basis of a working hypothesis.

Thus much at all events is clear, that we are speaking of a vastly greater extent of Space than that in which we move—a Space which is in absolute apposition with every point of our Space, not far away; on the contrary situated in such wise as that the smallest movement in the Fourth Direction would immediately bring us into it.

And this, that in that Space the mind is free to exercise itself in Four Directions instead of only three, and therefore finds its powers enormously increased, increased in proportion to the increase of the Space in which it works; for it is emancipated from the limitations which were imposed upon it in our Lower Space. Of these limitations we are not always conscious; to recognise the fact that they are due to the conditions of our Space requires a little thought. But it is to be hoped that the preceding discussion of the Lower Spaces has made this tolerably clear, for in truth there is no new principle involved.

VII

THE WORLD OF THE UNSEEN

I WILL call this Space The World of the Unseen.

This will at once suggest what is in my mind, viz. that it is not empty, not peopled only by imaginations and dreams, but full of life and activity, with all things that are necessary for the expression of that activity, and the maintenance and enjoyment of that life.

It is of necessity that the only proof that can be given in favour of this assumption must depend on circumstantial evidence, of which the force is largely cumulative. But this is no more than another way of saying that we are considering something that is out of reach. The same kind of proof is regarded as being valid in connection with other questions which deal with what is out of reach and out of sight; there is therefore no reason, so far, why it should not be the same in this case also.

The proof must consist in the answers which are given to questions such as these—

Does this theory explain what we know to be facts, though hitherto without explanation?

Does it remove any difficulties which have puzzled us?

Does it reconcile any apparent contradictions?

I hope and think that it does. And if this be shewn to be the case, the cumulative force of the argument will be largely increased by every additional success. Moreover, each case in which the theory is justified by its results, will present the thought of Higher Space in such a way as to tend to the satisfying of those who may have hesitated to receive it, on the ground that they cannot understand the conception, and do not regard the previous argument as being sufficient to establish the existence of a real Space beyond our Space, lying in an unknown direction, infinitely larger than our Space, and in perfect contact with it.

VIII

CONCERNING THE DEPARTED

WE have now seen some of the principles on which we are to depend, and are sufficiently equipped to proceed to the discussion of some of the questions which we are to consider.

The first of these is a very interesting one. It is this. Where do they dwell that are departed hence in the Lord? What is their condition?

These are questions which have received very many answers, and these answers by no means agree together.

When we speak of the Departed we are obliged to use the greatest caution; and I cannot think that our thoughts of them are even tolerably satisfactory.

We speak of them as being happy. We believe that they are in a state of happiness. We are right in doing so.

But while we are sure that they are happy, we are compelled to acknowledge that this conveys absolutely nothing to our minds as to the manner of their happiness.

The fact of their happiness is established. The manner of it is most obscure. There is a fundamental obstacle to the understanding of our words.

So far as saying that they are at peace, where the wicked cease from troubling and the weary are at rest, that they are in safe-keeping, in a better world, and so on, we are sure that we are making no mistake, because we receive these statements on the most certain warrant of Holy Scripture.

But when we come to think more closely about it, we find that so far as our description has gone, the happiness of which we have been speaking consists in the absence of disturbing elements, *i.e.* our description of it has been characterised by negatives.

Now we cannot understand a purely negative happiness. So long as we can only say that in their life there is not this or that to which we are accustomed, the only idea that is definitely presented to us is this, that their state is altogether different from anything with which we are acquainted, and each successive negative makes the distinction or even the contradiction between their state and ours more wide. So much so that the principle of Continuity which we have learnt to regard as being of almost, if not quite, universal application, fails us here.

It is true that in the case of one who regards GOD as his loving Father, his faith is able to surmount this difficulty. He is content to know that his departed are in the hands of a tender Father, Who is sure to fulfil His word to them, and give them all things that are necessary to their fullest happiness.

But this requires faith; and all men have not faith.

And even those whose faith is of the strongest and most robust would find a very true and lively satisfaction if they could only know something of the condition of their beloved ones who have gone from them.

We do want to know this, if it be possible; we do want to have something definite before us; something that we may be able to grasp if only partially; something that we may be able to understand, or at least begin to understand; something positive, or at least more positive than we have yet seen.

We want it, not for the vulgar reason of a devouring curiosity which desires to pry into everything that is concealed simply because it is concealed; not only in order that we may be able to think more intelligently of those who have gone before us, though this would be a legitimate and sufficient reason for such a desire; but also for our own sakes, that it may be possible for us to look forward in a more intelligent way with a more distinct anticipation to the time when we too shall depart hence and be no more seen in this world.

This want has long been felt; it has produced many attempts to describe the life of the other world. But some of them are very vague and very incomprehensible, adding in no degree to the understanding of the conditions of the other life; others again are of such a kind as not to be attractive to any save the most spiritually minded; while others are simply efforts to reproduce the scenery, the surroundings of this present life in its most lovely and delightsome aspects, investing them with the most glowing superlatives, yet leaving our thoughts no higher than our earthly material plane.

These two schools contradict each other.

It is not to be wondered at that this is so, indeed at present our ideas are in such a state of confusion that it could hardly be otherwise.

Let us begin at the beginning. There are, broadly speaking, two alternatives before us.

1. We may think of our departed brethren as being near to us. In this case we must regard them as being invisible,— *i.e.* unseeable, — and also intangible, for it is a matter of common experience that we do not see them, and cannot, as a rule, perceive their presence by any test. From this point of view we are compelled to suppose that they are immaterial, so far at least as our appreciation of matter is concerned; at all events they must be entirely different from ourselves.

2. On the other hand, we may think of them as enjoying an existence not wholly different from our own. This means that they are invested in some sort of material bodies, such as we can understand. In this case we are bound to think of them as being at a vast distance from us, a distance at all events sufficient to remove them from our sight, even when that is re-

inforced by all the appliances with which science has endowed us. Their habitation in this case may be supposed to lie in some one of the stars or planets, as some have thought, but it cannot be near to us.

In the present state of thought on this subject these two alternatives will practically exhaust the possibilities of the situation. For an ethereal or gaseous body, though it would technically answer to the description of a material form, is not such as we can contemplate with any satisfaction as a higher form of existence, nor can we comprehend, or even desire, the happiness of which, according to our appreciation, such a body would be susceptible.

Practically, I suppose, the majority of people are content to think of their departed as enjoying a real existence, *i.e.* real to their apprehension, without troubling themselves as to its character, and at the same time to regard them as being in some indefinable way near to them, though, as we have seen, the two things are incompatible; in a word they refuse to be influenced by a too rigorous attention to the logic of the case.

But how very unsatisfactory this is. There are two alternatives, mutually exclusive, but in effect both are accepted at the same time. Is it possible to imagine a more hopeless confusion of thought?

We will endeavour to enquire impartially what we do know of the departed, what firm ground we have to go upon. If we can but grasp some facts, some solid facts, surely they will help us to come to some definite conclusion, some distinct conception about our departed brethren who have gone before us, and their condition.

First, then, we have this Fact, that in the beginning GOD made man in His own Image, after His Likeness. He then gave to man the highest possible form.

This Likeness has not been entirely lost, however much it has been defaced by sin. Of this we are assured by the fact that the Son of GOD was able to take our nature upon Him when He came to dwell on Earth.

Man being therefore in the highest, noblest form, there is no higher nobler form that can be given to him.

That is when he leaves this world, and passes into a higher state of being, he retains the Likeness of GOD, or in other words, he still has a form at least analogous to ours. If it were otherwise, in a higher state of being he would take a lower form. This cannot be admitted for a moment.

So far we are supported by what S. John tells us in the Book of the Revelation, where we read that he saw the Redeemed clothed in white robes, wearing crowns on their heads, bearing palms in their hands, playing on instruments of music, and singing the new song.

Here a number of points are enumerated as having been observed by the Apostle. All of them are consistent with the idea that those whom he saw were seen under the likeness of humanity, and so far as I am aware there is no suggestion to the contrary to be met with in any authority on the subject; at all events there is nothing in the account of the vision which gives any reason to suppose that the Redeemed were noticeably different in their appearance from ourselves.

This too we may note, that S. John was not a careless observer, for the careful details which he gives us of the appearance of other beings which were very different from anything that he was accustomed to see, prove to us that he noticed accurately what was presented to his eyes.

We may therefore accept it as a fact that the Redeemed have forms analogous to ours, and that these forms are composed of some kind of material, which is a real material, even from the point of view of the unscientific man, a material which is not invisible or unseeable, for S. John did see them when he was in the position to do so.

Let this be called Fact A.

Side by side with this fact there is another which must be taken into consideration. It is this, that no one has ever seen a soul departing from the body; and that there are but few who even claim that they have seen a Spirit-form unless it has been, as they say, materialised.

This fact is in contradiction to the former fact. For if the departing soul is invisible to us, it cannot be material in such a sense as is required for our comprehension of its conditions.

It would therefore appear that the forms which S. John saw are to us invisible, that is, that it is impossible for us to see them. Let this be called Fact B.

To reconcile these two facts, A and B, without doing violence to either of them, or rather to find some conception which will include them both, is a task which is very difficult at present.

I suppose that the following will be accepted as a fair account of the usually received solution of the difficulty.

S. John was "in the Spirit." He therefore was able to see other spirits, but we cannot do so.

Pressing the question, Why not? we shall be told that a "spirit" is invisible to us, that a "spiritual" body cannot be seen except by "spiritual" eyes.

This cannot be accepted as a conclusive answer. What do we know of a "spirit" that we dare to say so positively that it is and must be invisible to us?

What is a "spirit"?

To answer that it is an existence, an essence, that it is ethereal, immaterial, impalpable, imperceptible by any tests, that for all we know the air may be full of "spirits," even thickly crowded with them, while we have no appreciation of their presence, all this is to veil in a cloud of words, and mostly negative, and if not negative very vague, the confession that we really know nothing about a "spirit," that a "spirit" is to us inconceivable, that we have no words by which to describe it, and in fact no clear ideas concerning it to be described.

Granting for a moment that this vague description is all that we can hope for, and that it is true as far as it goes, that this ethereal, rarefied, or immaterial existence has a form that can be recognised by its brother existences, we are still compelled to enquire, Of what kind are its pleasures? its functions? its means of expression?

To reply that the pleasures of a "spirit" are "spiritual" pleasures; that the functions of a "spirit" are "spiritual" functions; and the employments of a "spirit" are "spiritual" employments, is all that can be said. Of course it will be added that these "spiritual" evidences of life are far higher, far purer than those of which we have any experience; but that does not carry us any farther in the understanding of the conditions of spirits. Such amplifications are not elucidations, they are only comments, arising from a reverent desire to express the undoubted fact that the conditions of the departed in Paradise are better than ours here on Earth, while still leaving the question of the manner of their superiority unsettled. As a matter of fact all this tells us nothing, it simply leaves us where we were.

What we want is something definite, something that we may lay hold of. We cannot be really satisfied by the echoing backwards and forwards of the words "spirit" and "spiritual."

When we bless GOD'S Holy Name for those that are departed this life in His faith and fear, we want to have something in our minds for which we can thank Him intelligently, something that we may not only believe, but also understand to be better than what went before.

When we look forward to future happiness for ourselves, we want to see something before us which we can recognise as being better than what we have. In a word, we do want to know something about the conditions of the other world.

If this be proved to be impossible, we must be content to believe as we have believed, that those conditions are better than our present conditions; and to wait as we have waited, until we reach the farther shore.

But I cannot think that this is necessary. I am persuaded that it is possible for us to know a great deal about the conditions of the other world; I think that we have a right to expect this knowledge, and therefore I am sure that we do no wrong if we try to find out and formulate much concerning them.

Yet how can this reasonable desire be gratified so long as we have the two Facts A and B before us? One of them seems to describe an existence which is real to our comprehension, since it is not wholly different to our own; the other practically contradicts it, and gives only in its place, the words "spirit" and "spiritual" which we do not understand, which we cannot even begin to understand, which therefore represent what is to us an unreal existence.

By the first fact we are encouraged to believe that there is a real continuity between the present state of being and the future state, such as all experience of our progress, physical, mental, spiritual, leads us to expect. A development, an evolution it may be, but still, however great the advance, along the same lines as those to which we are accustomed.

The second fact seems to speak of a violent breach in this continuity, a tremendous dislocation, a revolution instead of an evolution, in all the aspects of our being. It demands a fresh start, from a new standpoint, in an entirely new state of things, in which "spirits," concerning which nothing can be predicated, pass their time in "spiritual" employments, performing "spiritual" functions, enjoying "spiritual" pleasures, all of which are of another order from anything with which we are acquainted, and therefore convey to our minds no idea at all.

I think that the idea of Higher Space supplies the necessary link between the facts A and B, and reconciles them.

We have understood that we cannot point in the direction of this Space, since it lies in the Fourth Direction which is unknown to us. We cannot by means of any of our senses penetrate into that Space, nor can any of our senses reveal to us anything that goes on within it. It is, however, to be reached from any point in our world, without passing through any other point in our world, by a movement in the Fourth Direction, which is first perceived when the limitations of the body are removed.

Suppose that the soul, when it parts from the body, passes into the Higher Space along the line of the Fourth Direction, and at once we find room for the two Facts A and B which before seemed to be opposed to each other, and even mutually exclusive.

This we proceed to shew.

The suggestion is that at the moment of dissolution the personality of the dying man is transferred into the Higher Space.

From what has been said above it appears that in the Higher Space there is an indefinitely extended expanse in which the true person of the man takes up its habitation. His powers and faculties are not lost. On the contrary they are infinitely increased, and as by our hypothesis this Higher Space is not empty but furnished with all that is necessary or even desirable for those who live in it, we are able to think of the departed as enjoying what is to our minds a real existence, with real forms, analogous to ours, and near to us. This gives room for Fact A.

The movement of the person in order to reach the Higher Space has been along an Unseen path into the Unseen World.

Therefore during the passage he is not seen. This gives room for Fact B.

Here, then, is a simple means of reconciling two facts which seemed to be in hopeless antagonism, a simple conception which includes them both, and exhibits them as being complementary to each other, instead of opposed to each other.

If now we think of our departed, we may rightly think of them as being in forms not wholly unlike our own; that is, forms such as we can consider as being real, not shadowy, nor immaterial; and at the same time we need not think of them as being at an infinite distance from us, although they are in a state in which all their powers are enormously, even infinitely increased, extended, and developed.

Here I must pause to guard against a possible misunderstanding or misconception. I am not to be understood as wishing to do away with the terms spirit and spiritual. The use of them is so common in Holy Writ that it is perhaps almost unnecessary to say so; but I do desire to protest emphatically against what I feel to be an abuse of these terms which gives the impression of something which we cannot recognise as being real, but on the contrary seems to describe what is very misty, very vague, and very much like a dream of the imagination.

I would submit that these words "spirit" and "spiritual" should be understood as describing a connection with Higher Space; while "body" and "bodily" describe a connection with our Lower Space.

It may be that some will think that this is rather premature, or at least that it is merely the substitution of one set of words for another. But I venture to hope that a greater familiarity with the thought of Higher Space will tend to the recognition of the fact that the substitution is of something thinkable for something unthinkable; of something concrete for something abstract; in a word, of something, however far beyond the reach of our senses, for what is practically no-thing.

In any case this is the sense in which the terms will be used in this essay, and therefore it is well that they should be defined as soon as possible. If it is found that this use of the words is not strained nor artificial, but natural, this will go a long way towards justifying it.

Now comes the question, Does this theory throw any light upon the condition of the Departed? Does it in any way enable us to comprehend anything of their state?

At all events this much has been arrived at, as we have proceeded, that we have seen a conceivable habitation for them in which we may think of them as dwelling in what are to us real bodies, with real powers, amid real surroundings, of which none are so utterly different from what we are accustomed to as that we cannot appreciate them.

This is so far satisfactory in itself; and since it agrees with what an unsophisticated mind would naturally expect (witness the beliefs of simple practical people like our far-off ancestors, and others), the satisfaction is increased.

Moreover, it agrees with the principle of Continuity, which leads us to expect that when the boundary of this world is passed the stream of life will not be violently interrupted or turned into another channel; and that the tendencies which have been blamelessly forming in our present life will not be reversed or thrown on one side as useless, but that all that is good will be preserved and strengthened.

Our theory tells us also that when one passes from us into the Higher Space, his sphere and power of action and sensation is indefinitely, even infinitely, enlarged. What is to us the unknown direction is perfectly well known to him, and all his faculties and aptitudes become adapted in accordance with this enlargement.

A little consideration will make the bearing of this evident. If we were to picture to ourselves such a condition as would be represented by perfect health of body and mind and soul, that, even in our World, our Space, would be most enviable. It would seem to offer such transcendently wonderful possibilities of growth and progress in knowledge, art, and grace, as to constitute a veritable Utopia.

But even so we should be compelled to recognise the existence of a bar to progress beyond a certain limit. Death places a boundary beyond which, in this stage of our existence, nothing can be touched. In this state of being, maturity is only the herald of decay; by accident, or it may be, by Euthanasia, the terminus of activity must sooner or later be reached even under the most favourable conditions imaginable.

This is a difficulty inherent in the very foundations of our physical existence. Our body, with its necessary infirmities, sets a limit even to our aspirations. In some cases the limit of time, in others the limit of endurance, in others again the limit of expression. However healthy the conditions may be, the mind, which is the more excellent partner in the firm, is constantly reminded of the imperfections of its associate the body; and strive how it may, it cannot educate it up to its requirements; however reluctantly, it is compelled to acknowledge that it cannot dissolve the partnership in this life, and must abide by the conditions of the association.

In the Higher Space this is no longer so, the weaker partner has been retired; the body, that is the mortal body, is no longer a drag on the mind, the corruptible elements have been shaken off, there is no more decay; death having done its utmost has but dissolved the partnership, and so removed the hindrance to farther progress.

And more, the condition of the Departed of whom we speak is rightly described as a holy state; and this qualification means nothing less than that they are in a condition of perfect health, and indefectible. All the diseases of the mind and soul are cured; and as time goes on the constitution itself, which has suffered during the time of probation here on earth, becomes stronger and stronger, instead of failing, as it does with us.

As a consequence boundless possibilities at once appear. Not only is the intellect set free from what has been a clog upon it, not only are the limits of time, endurance, and expression set back indefinitely, but more, far more, than that is found to have been accomplished.

Push back to the utmost limits the thought of what might be in this world under such conditions; let the mind revel in imagination of the potentialities revealed in such circumstances, still even such imaginations are totally inadequate to describe what is in Higher Space.

There, in the state of Greater Freedom, many of the complications which perplex us are seen to be but parts of a simple whole which we cannot discern. What are to us independent and isolated phenomena without any apparent connection with each other are plainly seen in their true and harmonious relationships. There, laws which have been painfully determined here, are seen to be no more than particular statements of special cases, easily to be deduced from higher laws which we cannot perceive. There, too, things which we regard as utterly impossible are not only natural, but matters of course; what we call miracles, of everyday occurrence.

The idea that the habitation of the Departed is at an infinite distance, or at least at a very great distance, is so ingrained in many minds that it is necessary to repeat that the Higher Space is not to be reached by gazing into the depths of our own Space. The telescope brings us no nearer. It lies close to us on every side. There is absolutely no distance between us and the boundary of that

Space. There is nothing which can interpose between us and the Higher Space.

Some gruesome stories of persons who have been buried alive recur to our memories. Enclosed as they were in shell, in lead, in casket, each made as carefully as possible, how does the spirit escape? Through these envelopes? Through the superincumbent earth? Not so. There is no barrier between them as they lie in the grave and the Higher Space. There is an open side of which we can know nothing save that it does exist, through which and by which the spirit passes into the Higher Space. A closed box is a prison from our point of view, but it is not so from the point of view of Higher Space.

This statement must be regarded as carrying us up to the limit of what can be said at present, but it is imperfect, and therefore we shall have to recur to this question later, when some further principles have been developed. Enough has been said, however, for us to recognise the immensity of the gain that comes to those who have departed this life in the faith and fear of GOD; and the vastness of the change which they experience, who, having learnt in this life that with all their studies, all their investigations, they can but know in part, and that a very small part, have now the door of higher knowledge opened wide before them, where they can enter in, and rejoice in their opportunities, and in their power of using them to the full.

IX

CONCERNING THE VISION OF THE RISEN LORD

Let us take two more facts, which, like the Facts A and B, appear at first sight to be in opposition to each other.

Our Blessed Lord, when He rose again from death, took again His Body with flesh, bones, and all things appertaining to the perfection of man's nature.

Still wearing that Body, He ascended up into Heaven, and there dwells, being now as truly in the form of man as He was while He walked the Earth.

Now the human Body of our Lord, with flesh, bones, and all things appertaining to the perfection of man's nature, cannot be invisible, *i.e.* unseeable, if It be within the range of vision. Real flesh on real bones must be visible if it be within the reach of sight. And as we have seen, the Risen Body of our Lord was and is a real body; for It was the same Body in which He went about, in which He suffered the pains of Death, that He took again, and not another or a phantasmic form.

S. Paul in 1 Cor. xv. details a number of appearances of our Lord after His Resurrection to various persons; then he adds, " Last of all He was seen of me also," using the same word to describe his own experience and that of those who saw Him during the Forty days between His Resurrection and His Ascension.

There is not the slightest suggestion that there was any difference in the kind of manifestation before and after the Ascension.

Again S. Stephen, having his eyes open, saw Him and knew Him. So did S. Paul, on his journey to Damascus. So did S. John in the great vision of the Apocalypse.[1] And among our most cherished beliefs is this, that we too, in the fulness of time, shall see Him, and know Him, the same Jesus Whom the Apostles saw going up into Heaven; and this—that He having entered Heaven as the Son of Man, has opened the Kingdom of Heaven to all believers among the sons of man.

Now, with regard to the two former of the Appearances which have been quoted, we note that they were vouchsafed to chosen men, not alone, but in the midst of many others. But they only saw Him. The rest of those standing round saw nothing. This is specially stated in the case of S. Paul, where we read that his companions heard a voice but saw no man. And in the other case the same conclusion is more than suggested, since from the course of the narrative it is evident that none of the meeting save S. Stephen saw the heavens open.

[1] See Note at the end of the Section.

We have then two facts which are in opposition to each other. The first that the Body of our Lord is a real Body. Let this be called Fact C.

The second that on two occasions He was seen by one man, while those who stood round did not and could not see Him. Let this be called Fact D.

How are these two Facts to be reconciled? or rather how are they to be explained together?

It is not enough to assume that the Resurrection Body of our Lord is a "spiritual" body in the common acceptation of the term, and to say that one of the properties of a spiritual body is that it can become visible or invisible at will. For the introduction of the word spiritual excludes Fact C altogether; since a spiritual body of which nothing can be predicated, nothing proved or disproved, is not what we understand by a real human body. And beside, seeing that we have no knowledge of any process by which a real human body can be at one and the same time visible to one person and not to other persons looking in the same direction, the "spiritual" supposition only introduces a new complication, instead of making the matter easier to understand. As a matter of fact, if It could do this It would not be what we mean by a true human body at all. And to endeavour to insist on this is to deprive words of their meaning, and to land us in a hopeless obscurity.

But if we bring the theory of Higher Space to bear, the two Facts C and D at once fall into line, and room is found for both of them.

Now we can understand that it was not the Body of the Lord that underwent a change, but that the change was effected by an additional power given to those who saw It; their eyes were opened, and the power of seeing into the Higher Space which was not imparted to their companions, was given to them for a special purpose. They were permitted to see what is. Even as S. John in the island of Patmos was permitted to see what is, though it is hidden from our eyes. Even as also the servant of the prophet Elisha was permitted to see what is, though we cannot see it.

All this follows naturally from the definition of the Higher Space, which teaches us that we cannot ordinarily see anything that is in that Space, because we do not know in what direction to look for it, and also because our senses are only adapted for use in our own Space.

Accepting this as a true definition, we are able to see how the real human Body of our Lord should be seen by some and not by others at the same time, without any unnatural imaginings as to visibility and invisibility as the property of a "spiritual" body.

This adds force to the results of the previous discussion, since now we are considering a Body not only formed of matter of some kind, concerning which we do not venture to dogmatise, of which we can only say that it is such as is real to us; but One of which we know that It is a real human Body, with all things appertaining to the perfection of man's nature. And this Body, may, as we have seen, be conceived as being in the Higher Space, the only place where we can think of It intelligently, while bearing in mind that It is near to us.

Remembering this there is far less difficulty in accepting the statements regarding the bodies and forms of the Departed, since we have found that the same principles as were quoted in their case are applicable in the case of an admittedly solid body.

NOTE

A very strong corroboration of our theory is to be found in Rev. i. 10, and iv. 1, 2, so strong indeed as to be almost startling.

This shews itself first of all in the repeated statement of S. John that on the two occasions, the former when he was privileged to see the Lord and to receive from Him the charge to write the Epistles to the

Seven Churches, the latter when he was permitted to be a witness of the Worship of Heaven, a change took place in him which he describes as being "IN THE SPIRIT" or becoming "IN THE SPIRIT."

Bearing in mind the definition given above as to the meaning of the word Spirit, this at once suggests that S. John was received into a Higher Space. Is this suggestion justifiable?

We will first run quickly through the various points which support this suggestion, and then add to the summary what may seem to be necessary.

j. Behold, a door opened in heaven, *i.e.* a means of access was perceived by which a new region migh be reached.

ij. This means of access was perceived by a new power of sight which was imparted to the observer, a power that was so wonderful that in comparison with it his sight at other times was blindness. The expression used is this, I SAW.

iij. Straightway, in obedience to the call come up hither, I was in the spirit, or as the Arabic version has it, I went in the spirit. The journey was of no long duration, for it was accomplished immediately, the distance was traversed in a moment.

We are able at once to interpret this.

The door represents the new Direction to which the Apostle had been insensible before, it was the Direction of a Higher Space.

The new power of vision was the power of perceiving the things in that region of Higher Space.

The journey was the short translation into Higher Space, which as we have seen is in immediate contact with our Space at every point.

It is not difficult to produce considerations in support of the foregoing.

j. The name of the Book in which we read these things is The Apocalypse. That is the Uncovering, or the Revelation. Taken in the natural sense, either of these words tells us that there was something that was uncovered, from which a veil was withdrawn. That is, that what was seen was real, not only a picture of what was real.

ij. The use of the verb to see in the intransitive voice followed by the word "behold" points in the same direction. This may be illustrated by a comparison with 1 Kings vi. 17, where in the LXX. the same use of the word is found. There we are able to recognise the full significance of the expression. For in that case we feel no doubt that what was seen by the servant of Elisha was real, and not only so, but that it was what he would have seen at any time, though perhaps not on so large a scale, if his eyes had been always open. What he saw was the Angelic guard that is stationed by our Father round about His people, His children, for their protection. This, as will be seen, in the Higher Space.

iij. With this may be compared the use of the word Seer, as applied at different times to prophets. Who by the power of GOD were enabled to see what was hidden from the eyes of others.

iv. The vision of the Adoration of heaven may be compared with the visions of Ezekiel and Isaiah, which are strikingly similar; this comparison tends to shew that what they all saw is what is going on constantly in heaven.

In order to accept these conclusions we have to get rid of a certain amount of prejudice, and that not of a merely modern date, for in Acts xii. 9 we read, "He wist not that it was true which was done by the angel, but thought he saw a vision." But this difficulty is not insuperable; more especially when we remember such expressions as the following, about the little book which in the course of the vision was eaten by S. John, "It was in my mouth as sweet as honey, and as soon as I had eaten it my belly was bitter." Here in the natural acceptation of the words we read a description of a real experience, that is when without prejudice we study the language of the text.

As a matter of fact it is not to be thought that a vision is in any sense unreal; there is already a distinction observed in the popular use of the expressions "vision" and "dream," at least to this extent that a "vision" is supposed to mean something more real than a "dream"; it is not of course always properly applied, but it is none the less recognised.

Speaking accurately, a vision is the seeing of something. The word is not a synonym for a dream or an imagination.

X

THE APPEARANCE OF OUR SPACE TO THOSE IN HIGHER SPACE

Before we proceed to the discussion of a third pair of facts, there is another principle which must be established.

It follows directly from the definition of Space of Four Directions. It is this, that to beings in the Higher Space our Space with all that it contains, presents itself as a thin film.

This is a very important point, which needs to be carefully considered.

By definition the World of the Unseen lies in an Unknown Direction. That is to say, we can draw no line which, however far produced, will penetrate into that Higher Space. If we could do so that Direction would not be unknown.

From this it follows that any straight line drawn in that Space towards our Space, will only pass through one point in our Space.

If it could pass through more than one point we should know its direction, since two points on a straight line are sufficient to determine the direction of that line.

Therefore, as we cannot determine the direction of any straight line passing through our Space to the Higher Space, such a line can only pass through one point in our Space.

Or in other words, a dweller in the Higher Space will look upon our Space as having only the ~~thickness~~ of one atom.

This is such a difficult conception that we will spend a little more time upon it. We must not expect to be able to realise exactly what this means in relation to ourselves; it is enough if we are content to know that it is so. We may try to help ourselves by saying that we present the same appearance to the dwellers in the Higher Space as any possible inhabitants of Space of Two Directions would present to us, but that does not take us much farther. The important thing is, not to understand, but to accept the principle which lies at the foundation of the conception of Higher Space, and then to use it and see whether or no the results which follow are such as recommend themselves to our intelligence.

The principle may, however, be illustrated in this way.

Suppose that one end of a rod were placed against a small aperture in a partition, in such a way as that only the extremity should be visible, then the rod itself might be turned about in any way by a person behind the screen, while we should have no power of saying what position it occupied at any time. One point only of the rod is seen by us, and that gives no indication of the position of the rest of it.

From the point of view of dwellers in the Higher Space we have our physical existence actually in the partition which is of an indefinitely small thickness to their perception, not of course mathematically a plane or surface, since that has no thickness at all, but physically to be regarded as of the thickness of an atom; that is, practically the thickness of a soap-bubble just before it bursts. This being our situation, the rod of which we spoke may be turned about in an infinite number of directions, while we, who are only able to see one point of it, are unconscious of any change of position.

We are not now concerned with any questions as to the position of ourselves with regard to this film, whatever that may be it does not affect us in any way, what we are, we are; and the fact that we appear to others in a fashion different from that in which we are accustomed to think of ourselves does not alter or change our present position, though it may lead us to see that it is not necessarily such as we have thought it to be; and even though the idea presented to us may and does seem very strange, still it is no more than a translation of the fact which was noted before, that the Higher Space is contiguous to every point in a Lower Space, the which was definitely proved first in passing from Space of One Direction to Space of Two Directions; next in passing from Space of Two Directions to Space of Three Directions, and then in passing from Space of Three Directions to Space of Four Directions.

It is no doubt a strange conception, contrary to all our ideas about ourselves, contrary to our ideas about our Space, our Universe, which stretches away so far in Three Directions, and seems to be so large in all directions with which we are acquainted; but for all that there can be no doubt as to the truth of what has been stated, and the fact that we cannot understand it is not to be wondered at, since if we could do so we should have escaped from the limitations of our Space, and the Fourth Direction would be known.

The results of the application of this principle are very far-reaching, as we shall see in a short time; but even the nearest, which is obvious, is of great value; for at once we perceive a measure of the exceedingly Greater Freedom of those who, having been transferred from our Space into the Higher Space, now regard their past conditions and surroundings as being so cramped and circumscribed. The enlargement of which they are so happily conscious is made more evident to us by the comparison.

To this enlargement, this Greater Freedom, we too look forward. And if for no other reason than this, that we are thus enabled to figure to ourselves a rational idea of this Greater Freedom, it is worth while to try to familiarise our minds with this representation of our present state, and become acquainted with the narrowness of our present bounds.

But there is more than this to be learnt from the application of this principle, as we shall now proceed to shew.

XI

THE MINISTRY OF THE ANGELS

LET us consider the ministry of the Angels.

In this case as before we are confronted by two facts which *a priori* seem to be opposed to each other.

The former of these two facts is this, that the Angels are concerned in our affairs, and give assistance to us, having received a charge concerning us to keep us in all our ways, lest at any time we dash our foot against a stone. Let us call this Fact E.

The second Fact is this, that we never see an Angel, and that we never consciously feel an Angel's touch. Let us call this Fact F.

In this case the explanation that the forms of Angels are "spiritual" forms, and their bodies "spiritual" bodies, and their ministrations "spiritual" ministrations, does not really shew itself. For if the Angels are such that we cannot feel their touch, what can they do for us in any physical sense at all?

The practical acknowledgment of this difficulty is to be seen in the very slight importance that is attached, popularly, to the ministry of the Angels; and how clearly the difficulty is recognised is shewn in this that the idea of Angelic interposition in our affairs is largely treated as superstitious, and that in spite of Fact E. This is evidently wrong, for there are few things more clearly to be read in the Bible than this, that our Father does send His servants the Angels to minister to us His children.

But how are we to receive the two Facts E and F at the same time?

Again the theory of Higher Space

offers the answer. The sphere of the operations of the Angels is, generally speaking, in Higher Space. We cannot therefore see them, nor can we, according to our definition, feel their touch, since our senses are only adapted for the perception of sensations coming to us in our own Space.

It is not, however, necessary that even physically we should imagine ourselves open only to influences coming to us in our Space. We have seen that every particle of our bodies is in the most immediate contact with Higher Space. From thence then the Angels may touch us and bear us up in their hands, while yet we are unconscious of their touch as a touch, only being able to recognise it by its effects. They have touched us in such a way as no person or thing in our Space can touch us; therefore we have not recognised the touch by any feeling that we know; it has been applied on a side which we know not, and still it has been effectual.

XII

SO FAR THE PROPOSITION HAS NOT PROVED UNREASONABLE

So far then the theory that it is in Higher Space that we shall find a solution of many difficulties has stood its ground.

Three pairs of facts A and B, C and D, E and F, which at first sight appeared to be in antagonism as regards their components, have joined hands, and are seen to be in harmony with each other.

It may be said with confidence that it is not unreasonable to describe the Higher Space as the abode of our Departed brethren, of the Angels, and of our Lord Himself. That in this way we may rationally think of our Departed brethren as being in forms at least analogous to our own; with powers not of an utterly different character from our own, though very highly developed; with opportunities of employment and enjoyment suited to those powers, and therefore not wholly beyond our understanding. That it is not unreasonable to think of the Angels, great in power and might, as having their habitation in the Higher Space, from which and in which they both can and do assist us in accordance with our Father's will. That it is not unreasonable to think of our Lord Himself, still in the form of man, with all things appertaining to the perfection of man's nature, as dwelling in the Higher Space, and as being actually present with us when we are met together in His Name, as He has promised, though we cannot see Him.

If it be objected that all this depends on an unknown Direction, let it be considered that, if it were pretended that there was nothing unknown about it, the theory would stand self-condemned, since we are dealing with the unknown. And farther, that if this unknown direction, which at least is definite and confined to the one direction, helps us to understand something of what is not only unknown but also indefinite, it has strong claims on our attention. Moreover, this is but one unknown, whereas before there were many; and this unknown brings harmony where there was nothing but confusion beforetime.

If these three points were all in which the theory could help us, it might not unreasonably be suspected still. But if it shall be found that it is of great assistance to us in a variety of other ways, we shall have a greater confidence in it.

XIII

CONCERNING THE OMNISCIENCE OF ALMIGHTY GOD

LET us now apply our theory to the consideration of far higher problems.

Take the last principle that has been quoted, that to an inhabitant of the Higher Space this world and all that it contains is seen as a thin film, so that every part of it is open to inspection.

GOD dwells in Higher Space.

Here then we have a comprehensible interpretation of the fact that to Him all hearts are open, all desires known, from Him no secrets hid, since thus all things are seen to be naked and opened to Him with Whom we have to do.

This statement may seem to be imperfect, since, so far as we have gone, it is only with physical questions that we have concerned ourselves; and it might well appear that molecular changes do not account for all that goes on within us, in our hearts, etc.; but putting this aside for the present with the intention of returning to it later, we may note that this way of looking at the Omniscience of GOD takes us a step farther back than any other view of the matter, and gives us a reason of the faith that is in us as to the perfect Knowledge of all things which we are accustomed, and rightly accustomed, to associate with the mind of GOD.

To speak of Him as the Unconditioned, is to use a phrase which, however true it is, is terribly hard to realise; to regard Him as pervading all things, and penetrating all things in virtue of His Almighty power, is a conception which is difficult indeed to grasp; to think of Him as a "Spirit" in the ordinary acceptation of the word, to Whom all things are possible—

because we cannot know what a "spirit" is, and therefore cannot deny anything that may be said about it—is to involve ourselves in obscurity.

But when we are able to see HOW He is infinitely near to every point of everything in Heaven and in Earth, then the cloud that rested over our ideas of Him is lifted, and we are able, at least in some degree, to understand how it is that He knows all things; to perceive how His attribute of Omniscience arises.

XIV

YET HIGHER SPACES

So far I have been speaking in a general way of Higher Space; carefully avoiding the mention of the Fourth Direction as far as possible, after the time when the principles were enumerated which the first consideration of it yielded to us.

I have done this for two reasons. First because it was desirable to complicate matters as little as possible; and secondly because by refraining from more particular expressions it was possible to present the arguments based on the three pairs of Facts A and B, C and D, E and F together.

But now at this point it is necessary to go farther, and to recognise a very wide extension of the idea of Higher Space, which is by no means exhausted when we have reached the conception of Space of Four Directions.

There is no new difficulty introduced; when we have accepted the idea of a Fourth Direction in addition to the Three with which we are acquainted, the Higher Directions follow easily. Or in other words, when we have recognised the existence of Space of Four Dimensions there is no greater strain called for in the recognition of the existence of Space of Five Dimensions, and so on up to Space of an infinite number of Dimensions.

The same methods which have led us from Space of One Direction through Space of Two Directions, from thence to Space of Three Directions, and through that to Space of Four Directions, will lead us on to Space of Five Directions, and so on indefinitely.

The same principles that we have

observed concerning the relation of Space of Two Directions to Space of One Direction, the relation of Space of Three Directions to that of Two, the relation of Space of Four Directions to that of Three, hold good with regard to the relations of Space of Five Directions with Space of Four Directions, and so on indefinitely.

To think therefore of Space of many more Directions than Four calls for no new effort. When the first step has been taken the others follow naturally.

Each Space then in the ascending scale of numeration is in the most immediate juxtaposition with every point in the next Lower Space. Or translating this in the general case as we have done in a special case, it comes to this, that to one dwelling in a Higher Space the Space immediately below it in order appears as a thin Film, in which all objects occupy the whole thickness of the Film. And though it is impossible even to begin to imagine what the appearance of a material object in our Space may be to an observer in a much Higher Space, still it is evident that to him is presented a still more infinitely perfect view of its constituents than to an observer in any Lower region of Space. While to an eye in the Highest Space of all, an infinitely perfect revealing of the most hidden and secret things is of necessity presented.

This emphasises very strongly what has been said about the Omniscience of GOD. For He, dwelling in the Highest Space of all, not only has this perfect view of all the constituents of our being, but also is most infinitely near to every point and particle of our whole constitution. So that in the most strictly physical sense it is true that in Him "we live and move and have our being."

And then, regarding GOD as dwelling in the Highest Space of all, by the simple recollection of our definition that each Space is to those dwelling in an Inferior

Space in an unknown direction, we understand how it is that none can see GOD, that none can reach His dwelling-place, nor know where it is situated, while yet He is absolutely near to us.

XV

CONCERNING THE OMNIPOTENCE OF GOD

BUT this is not all. We have seen something of the manner of the Omniscience of GOD, and of His Omnipresence. Now if we make use of one of the principles which we noted from the beginning, we learn something of the manner of His Omnipotence.

It will be remembered that in discussing the conditions and the state of the Departed, we saw that they are freed from the limitations which of necessity are associated with our Lower Space. Many of our disabilities no longer exist for them, they are no longer subject to the restrictions of our Lower World. Assuming that they have passed into the next Higher Space, they are adapted for an existence in which there is room for expression in Four Directions instead of only Three, and energies proportionate to this higher opportunity of expression are theirs. Their powers and faculties are indefinitely increased by the removal of the finite bounds which not only enclosed them but cramped and hindered their expansion ; now they find room for vast development.

Pursuing the same thought as we rise in imagination through the series of Higher Spaces, this appears, that in each successive ascending Space, all the disabilities peculiar to the next below it in order are removed, all restrictions special to that Lower Space are shaken off.

Step by step that which existed receives a more perfect development, that which was latent becomes patent, that which was potentiality becomes accomplished, that which was in the germ advances towards maturity, until at last in the Highest Space of all, where GOD Himself Alone is found, all limitations of whatever kind are swept away, and that which has been growing towards the Highest, receives its illimitable, its absolute perfection, in the Person of GOD HIMSELF, in Whom dwells infinite Power and Knowledge, and Wisdom, to Whom be Glory and Dominion for ever and ever.

Thus led, from step to step, from our own Space, which to our senses and perceptions is of infinite extent, onwards and upwards through Higher Infinities till we reach the Absolute, the Infinite Infinity, a more true because more real appreciation of what GOD is, is presented to us; and though we fail, as we must fail, to grasp it, seeing that we are but finite creatures, a reasonable view of His Attributes, Omniscience, Omnipotence, and Omnipresence, is set before us, and that in such a way as to enable us to realise the fact that we, at the foot of the scale at present, are yet partakers of the Divine Nature and shall, by His grace, in His Own good time, be raised to be with Him, and like Him.

These steps are of great value to us; for though they be so great, still they afford a series of resting-places for our thoughts as they rise up to GOD, supplying thus a need which all must have experienced, who, meditating on the Being of GOD, have found no place to dwell on between themselves and Him.

Before leaving this part of our subject we must observe that one of the finite limitations of our Space stands in the way of our accepting it, or at least in the way of our full appreciation of it.

We are accustomed to think of individual intelligence as being concentrated in one point, or at all events in one person who occupies a very small portion of our Space. This is perhaps inevitable, since our unit of intelligence is one man.

Still, if we wish to grasp the significance

of the conception of the Omniscience of GOD, we must divest ourselves of this impression.

Intelligence and consciousness are set free in the Higher Regions, they are not confined as they are here. And as will be seen later, even in our own case the impression is hardly a true one.

Enlarging, therefore, our ideas, we must regard GOD, The Intelligence, The Consciousness, not as though the Mind of GOD were located in one place, but rather as being where He is, and that is everywhere.

We must not allow ourselves to think of Him as if there were some centre of His Mind, but on the contrary we must conceive of It as embracing all things, and as having neither centre nor circumference.

XVI

DEFENDING THE USE OF GEOMETRY IN THESE SACRED CONNECTIONS

Here I must interrupt the current of our thoughts, to obviate the charge that may be made, that it is irreverent to use the terms of Geometry in speaking of such awful subjects as the Being and Attributes of Almighty GOD.

I am conscious of no irreverence, but very humbly seek to use all the means which have been given to me, so as to gain a greater knowledge of Him Who is the Giver.

Theology—and this is the aim of every true system of Theology, to teach us more of GOD—is the Queen of sciences, and therefore has the undoubted right to call them all to serve her, as servants, not as rivals, which they can never really be. If they can serve their Queen, they take their true position, and occupying that, while they are honoured, she suffers no loss.

XVII

OUR RELATION TO THE DWELLERS IN THE HIGHER SPACE

I NOW come to a point which I postponed.

1. Speaking of the ministry of the Angels, I said that every part of our bodies is open on two sides to the inhabitants of the next Higher Space. With this thought we are now familiar.

While this is true, it is, however, only a part of the truth. It was a preliminary statement, which must now be supplemented. The distinction between our bodies and ourselves must not be forgotten. Our body is not the only constituent of our being; that is composed, as we are aware, of body, soul, and spirit, and of these the body is of the least consideration.

Would it then be true to say that to the eye of an inhabitant of Higher Space we ourselves appear as Films?

The answer to this question depends upon the answer to another, which is this, Where are our spirits now? This is an enquiry which has long waited for an answer. Will our theory help us in this matter?

I think it will. Indeed the use of the word Spirit, if the definition given above be true, viz. that a Spirit is in connection with, and belongs to Higher Space, affords at least a hope that we may find some light thrown upon the difficulty.

The suggestion is evidently this, that even now our Spirits are in the Higher Space.

It is not difficult to find many considerations which point in this direction.

Seeing that when man was first formed he was made in the Image of GOD, and still retains something of that Likeness which was originally impressed upon him, it is hardly possible to imagine that we ourselves appear to the inhabitants of the next Higher Space otherwise than in that Likeness. Our bodies indeed would appear as Films, but since the Divine Image was given to the whole man, and not to his body only, we are not confined to the supposition that that Image appears only in our physical presentment; on the contrary, we must acknowledge that it was imprinted no less on our soul and spirit. And therefore—since otherwise we should have to imagine that the Divine Likeness is degraded in the eyes of those in the next Higher Space into the appearance of a Film —we are led to this, that they see us, that is, our higher nature, in that Image.

It is not a perfect image, only too often in truth it is distorted most painfully by sin or by neglect; but yet in such wise that some remains of past glories may be traced in it. In other words, we conclude that the higher parts of us are even now in

Higher Space, confined it is true to the boundaries of our Space by reason of their connection with the body, but still outside our Space from our point of view.

On these, which we may crudely call our characters, the eyes of those who dwell in Higher Space are turned, and they perceive our likeness to GOD in them more or less plainly according to the Grace which we have received and used.

This means that we have a real spiritual body as well as a physical body. And that while one of them, the physical, the lower of the two, is confined to our Lower Space, the higher is not so confined. That is outside our Space. And the relation of the Lower body to the Higher is that of a section to a solid figure, by which it is enclosed, with which it is in the most intimate relationship. This relation subsists until Death snaps the bond which unites the two, and, setting free the Higher body from the Lower, enables it to depart into the region of the Greater

Freedom which is its true inheritance, and enjoy it. The personality suffering no diminution, but rather, as we have seen, becoming more stable by reason of its translation into the Higher World.

Thus from the point of view suggested by our theory, it appears that we are not to regard the soul or spirit as being in any sense contained in the body, but rather as containing it; while also we are taught to perceive more clearly the relative importance of the two.

These two bodies are for the present in large measure mutually dependent, and are very closely allied in our present state. Only too often the Higher body, *i.e.* the spiritual, is compelled by the Lower body, *i.e.* the physical or natural, to take the lower part in the determination of questions in the interest of the partnership; to postpone its interest to the lower interests, to give up its aspirations in favour of earthly desires, till the life of the spiritual body may become stunted, dwarfed, and starved, even reduced to a pitiable state of weakness, owing to the rapacity of the demands of its coarser associate.

The words which I have just used to describe the relations of what I am regarding as two actual bodies, the one in our Space, the other in the Higher Space, using them therefore with perfect literalness, are words which might most naturally be used by any one who wished to describe a man on the downward path; the only difference being, though it is an essential one, that he would use them metaphorically, whereas I hold that they describe a real state of things in which two actual bodies are at issue between themselves.

This, however, is no objection. If this conception of Higher Space exhibits as being in truth realities what have been considered as metaphors or illustrations, that is to its credit, not the reverse.

2. A statement such as this must not be based upon mere argument. We are

bound to enquire what we may learn from Holy Scripture on this point. By this it will stand or fall.

Here we shall have to go into very considerable detail.

S. Paul's great chapter on the other world, part of which is familiar to most of us as being read at the Burial of the dead, 1 Cor. xv., is the passage to which we naturally turn in the first place, and there in v. 40, we read, "There are also celestial bodies, and bodies terrestrial; but the glory of the celestial is one, and the glory of the terrestrial is another."

Reading these words literally, with the thought that is before us in our minds, there is an evident agreement between the theory and one aspect of S. Paul's statement.

But in such a connection we must go farther than this, and find either here or elsewhere a stronger corroboration than this.

It must be shewn that the view which I have taken is one that receives more than an *a priori* support, based on a desire to find support in any place.

First then we observe that although the mention of "celestial bodies" is immediately followed by a statement about the sun, moon, and stars, nobody supposes that they are the celestial bodies of which the Apostle is thinking. In v. 41, in which he mentions the sun and moon and stars, he is simply taking up again the line of v. 39, and, continuing his description of the various kinds of existence with which we are more or less acquainted, points out that there are many different ranks or orders in the creation of GOD; his object being to shew that apart from revelation it is not hard to come to the conclusion that there are other ranks and orders beyond what we can see.

Of course, the main point before his mind was the doctrine of the resurrection of the body; and writing to those whose faith in the resurrection was still young, and beside that, disturbed by some who said that there was no resurrection of the dead, he wished to make the doctrine as clear as possible, whether by illustration, by invoking the principle of continuity, as well as by more open argument, and appeal to the Resurrection of Christ Himself.

Still this object by no means necessarily interfered with his giving a parenthetical glance at a nearly related subject, nor did it prevent him, here any more than elsewhere, from setting down a luminous definition on the related subject by the way. I take it that v. 40 is to be regarded as such a definition, none the less valuable because it is not strictly in connection with what went before and follows it.

In order to arrive at a distinct understanding of this verse I shall set down all the places where the word translated "celestial" is to be found.

They are these :—

Matt. xviii. 35.—My *Heavenly* Father.
John iii. 12.—If I have told you earthly things,

and ye believe not, how shall ye believe when I tell you of *Heavenly* things?

1 Cor. xv. 40.—There are *Celestial* bodies, and bodies terrestrial: but the glory of the *Celestial* is one, and the glory of the terrestrial is another.

1 Cor. xv. 48, 49.—As is the earthy, such are they that are earthy: and as is the *Heavenly*, such are they also that are *Heavenly*. And as we have borne the image of the earthy, we shall also bear the image of the *Heavenly*.

Eph. i. 3.—The Father Who hath blessed us with all spiritual blessings in *Heavenly places* in Christ Jesus.

Eph. ii. 6.—Hath raised us up together, and made us sit together in *Heavenly places* in Christ Jesus.

Eph. iii. 10.—That now unto the principalities and powers in *Heavenly places* might be made known, by the Church, the manifold wisdom of GOD.

Eph. vi. 12.—We wrestle not against flesh and blood, but against principalities, against powers, against the rulers of Darkness of this world, against spiritual wickedness in *High places*. R.V. Heavenly places.

Phil. ii. 10.—Things in *Heaven*, and things in earth, and things under the earth.

2 Tim. iv. 18.—Will preserve you unto His *Heavenly* kingdom.

Heb. iii. 1.—Partakers of the *Heavenly* calling.

Heb. vi. 4.—The *Heavenly* gift.

Heb. viii. 5.—The example and shadow of *Heavenly* things.

Heb. ix. 23.—The *Heavenly* things.

Heb. xi. 16.—They desire a better country, that is, a *Heavenly*.

Heb. xii. 22.—The *Heavenly* Jerusalem.

These are, I think, all the passages in which this word is to be found. And among many other points of interest which are nearly related to our subject, this stands out at present in the greatest prominence, that it will be seen from reading them that there is no reason whatever for taking the words in 1 Cor. xv. 40 as if they stood thus, " There is a terrestrial body and there *will be* celestial bodies." For the word " heavenly " is used to qualify things and persons existing in the past and in the present as well as in the future.

It will also be observed that there is a very close connection between the words "spiritual" and "heavenly," especially in the contrast which is shewn between what is represented by either of them, and what is represented by the word earthy.

I would therefore submit that we should understand by this word that we are considering "belonging to Higher Space." By doing so we shall lose nothing in any of the passages quoted, on the contrary a more definite meaning is given to them. And in particular one passage, Eph. vi. 12, receives a meaning which entirely obviates the shock which is occasioned by thinking of Spiritual wickedness in *Heavenly* places. Now we may think of this spiritual wickedness as finding a home in Higher Space indeed, but not in the Highest to which alone the title Heaven properly belongs; a shock which induced our earlier translators to substitute "high places" for heavenly places in the Authorised Version of the passage, though in the Revised Version we find the reading "heavenly places" transferred from the margin to the text.

[It may be of interest to note here that in the Versions of 1380, 1534, 1539 we find "Heavenly things"; in 1557 "Things which are above"; in 1582 "In the Celestials"; in 1611 "In High Places," which shews that the translators felt the apparent incongruity of the expression, and gradually edged away from the literal translations of older times.]

It may be said with truth that, granting that these heavenly bodies have present existence in the Higher Space, there is another explanation which may be given, to wit that these are the bodies of the Departed of which we have spoken before, and it may be felt that this is the natural meaning of the words.

There is, however, no difficulty in combining this view with the other, that we have even now "heavenly" bodies in the Higher Space, the which, though they are still connected with our earthly bodies, are of the same kind as those of the Departed.

When we consider other passages, this seems to be at least a probable supposition.

The first of these passages comes from

the same chapter, 1 Cor. xv. 44. "There is a natural body and there is a spiritual body." This, standing alone, points in the same direction as v. 40; but v. 49 has a very important bearing on our subject, and at first sight seems to exclude the view which I am taking, reading as it does, "As we have borne the image of the earthy, we shall also bear the image of the heavenly."

But there are a great many ancient authorities which read, "Let us bear the image of the heavenly," so many in fact that the Revised Version gives this in the margin as a possible if not a probable amendment; while Drs. Westcott and Hort have adopted this reading in their text, giving the ordinary reading only in the margin.

This goes a long way towards my object; for even if the reading is disputed, there is no higher authority than that which I have quoted; and at the worst, from my point of view, the passage is neutralised so as not to be of weight against my contention, even if it is not to be quoted in my support.

Further it may be observed that much of the criticism which has declined to read "let us bear" is based upon the ground that S. Paul's treatment of the subject is physical, while "let us bear" is wholly ethical.

This criticism is disarmed when a physical or even a quasi-physical meaning is found in the exhortation which, as we are regarding it, urges us to the development of a spiritual body, a real physical body in the Higher Space, real, though not the same as our bodies in this Lower Space.

Consider some other passages such as these: "Our citizenship is in Heaven." "We are fellow-citizens with the Saints and of the household of GOD." "Ye are come to the heavenly Jerusalem, and to an innumerable company of Angels—to the spirits of just men made perfect."

These passages speak definitely of a

real and actual relation between the Departed and ourselves, such as our Lord described when He prayed to His Father, that not only they who believed on Him, but also those who should believe on Him through their word, might be joined together in perfect oneness; that is, in the relationship to our belief in which we testify when in the Creed we declare that we believe in the Communion of Saints.

3. This then appears from our present point of view, that what is true of the Departed in the other world is also true of us, so far as is possible under our conditions, which confine us within narrow limits, not indeed exclusively to our own Space, but to an area at no great distance beyond it. That is, that our Higher Nature finds its abode in the Higher Space, and its expression—impeded indeed and embarrassed by the mortal body which ties it to the neighbourhood of our Space, and infects it with some of its imperfections,

but yet in actual reality subsisting in the Higher Space — in the likeness of our departed brethren.

They are free from these embarrassments, while we are waiting the time of freedom, but yet, with the necessary limitations which are imposed on us, what is true of them is also true of us.

Very many of the expressions which are in common use to describe progress in the spiritual life are such as lend themselves freely to this conception. We speak of the growth of our spiritual powers in the same terms as we use to describe the growth of our bodily and mental powers, and though we may do so with the feeling that this is only because we have no other terms of which we may avail ourselves, it is at least possible to suppose that these terms are really descriptive of what is actually the case, viz. that taken literally they do describe a similar process of development in our mental and spiritual bodies in the Higher Space. Thus the anthropomorphic language of books, dealing with the Higher Life, is not due to the poverty of our means of expression, but affords the only true description of the phenomena which go on in connection with us in the Higher Space.

There are three expressions which bear on this conception. They speak of us as "going from strength to strength," as "receiving grace for grace," as "being changed from glory to glory," and so being transformed by steps into the glory of the Lord.

These passages and many others seem to point to a still larger development of our theory. Namely this, that it is not only in Space of Four Directions that our Bodies of Extension have existence, but rather that as we rise in the scale of Grace so also we rise in the scale of Space.

Remembering that to reach even the Highest Space of all there is no need to pass through any Lower Space, since each

Space, however high in order, is in immediate apposition to our Space, it appears that both we whose physical bodies are confined to our region of Space, and the Departed who are freed from that Space, and raised above it, have Bodies of Extension in the Higher Spaces. And that growth in grace is, we might say, physically represented in the Higher Spaces by the appearance and development in them of spiritual bodies, absolutely connected in our case with our mortal bodies, and so tied down to the more immediate neighbourhood of our Space, and in the case of the Departed, restricted to the boundaries of the Space in which they have their habitation.

And passing from ourselves and our likeness to the Departed, this seems to be suggested in regard to the Saints at Rest, that as they grow in grace and knowledge they are successively set free from the limitations of Lower regions, and advanced into the Higher Spaces, thus drawing nearer to the Highest, and being endowed with Higher powers, and more developed and higher capabilities of service.

Thus, step by step, the Freedom becomes greater and greater still, till in the end, when the consummation of all things has issued in the final rehabilitation of our Nature, when we have been made like unto the Lord in His Resurrection Body, our body having received that redemption for which we groan,—having, that is, been set free from the limitations and trammels of this Lower Space—the Greater Freedom becomes perfect and indefectible, and we, reconstituted in the Image of GOD as at the first, shall have received the Crown of our then glorified human nature, in the presence of our Father.

But this is by the way, and there are other passages which bear upon our relation to Higher Space which must be quoted. Such as these, "Where thy treasure is there will thy heart be also." "Set your affection on things above, not on things on the earth for . . . your life is hid with Christ in GOD."

Heart; affection; life; all spoken of as having a home in the Higher State, or rather, as we should say, in the Higher Space.

The same may be observed of such places as these, " Risen with Christ," " Partakers of His Resurrection," which seem to tell of a real connection with His life, the which as we have seen is to be thought of as in the Higher Space.

Here too is a most suggestive expression from S. Paul, he speaks of "your members *which are on the earth.*" This surely tells of members of ours which are not on the earth, members as real as our earthly members, which are in real union with us, although in the Higher Space.

With this may also be taken the thought that we are members of Christ, which tells of a higher connection with Him, a higher likeness to Him than can be found in our members which are on the earth. A likeness not only in character, but far more true than that, existing and shewing itself plainly and unmistakably to those who dwell in the Higher Space. With this passage may be taken one of those which was quoted above, "As is the Heavenly such are they that are heavenly," which describes a similarity not to be perceived by any of our Lower senses here in this world of ours.

In harmony with all this is the petition in the Collect for Ascension Day, in which we pray that "like as we do believe our Lord Jesus Christ to have ascended into the heavens, so we may also in heart and mind thither ascend, and with Him continually dwell"; a petition which is in perfect agreement with many other passages.

A considerable number of passages have now been brought under consideration, and in no case has any violence been done to them in using them to support our theory.

Wild though it may appear at first sight, there is nothing to condemn it in any of the passages quoted, nor have words been torn from their context, in order that they might be pressed into the service of a preconceived idea.

This then may represent the conclusions arrived at. That men of high character, of exalted aims, whose thoughts are lofty, whose hearts are raised above this world, whose desires are elevated, whose affection is set on things above, have spiritual members in heavenly places, that is, real Bodies of Extension in Higher Space, Higher according to their advancement and growth in grace. And on the other hand that men whose nature is debased, whose aims and thoughts and desires are low, who have dishonoured the Likeness of GOD in themselves, and become earthly, sensual, devilish, do not appear at all in the Higher Spaces, but are confined to the lower regions of Space.

Before passing on farther, we may

notice how easily our language lends itself to the needs of our theory, and even suggests, by means of common expressions, various thoughts connected with it. It is tempting to go into details on this point, but as this is not essential to our argument the temptation must be resisted.

XVIII

OUR HIGHER FACULTIES, OR HIGHER SPACE SENSES

THE next question which presents itself is one regarding our higher capacities. If we really have those Bodies of Extension in the Higher Spaces, what are the powers with which they are endowed, and what evidence have we as to the existence of those powers? If it is true in any sense that we have a share in the life of the Higher Spaces, what is our share in it?

It must not be forgotten that our Bodies of Extension are rigidly confined to the immediate neighbourhood of our own Space, so that the share they have in the life of Higher Space is not as yet a very large one. Further that whether of necessity, or by reason of habit, the mortal body being the medium of expression for most of our powers, these powers are dependent on it in a very large degree for their manifestation; and its resources of interpretation, whether by word or deed, are inadequate for such a task, which therefore can only be inadequately performed.

Yet of three Higher Space capacities at least we know the names, and something more.

Faith is one, Hope is another, and Love the third and greatest.

These are not of the earth earthy, they have another origin. Love, the chief of them, is even of the highest origin, for GOD is Love, and Love comes down to us from GOD and from no lower source; being imparted to us as one of the marks of His Own Likeness.

Of all our powers it is true that GOD has given them to us, but of those that find their field of exercise in lower regions, *i.e.* in our world exclusively, we may say, without hesitation, that they are lower than those that do not confine their activities to our Space.

Take then these three. They certainly do not confine themselves to our Space. False simulacra of them, bearing their names, especially of the Highest, Love, are to be found, which are and must be confined to lower regions. But they themselves cannot be so confined.

True Love extends beyond our present boundaries, embraces those who have passed from us, not only their memories, and farther than that it reaches, till it extends to GOD Himself.

This is no earth-born power, it is an attribute of our Bodies of Extension in the Higher Space, although it has its manifestations in this world of ours, which glow with more than earthly lustre.

We are ourselves accustomed to declare of Love that it is eternal, thus we assert that it does not belong to temporal things.

We speak too of Love as being Divine, *i.e.* GOD-like; and GOD Himself, describing His Love for us, has not shrunk from expressing that highest form of Love in terms of the Love of an earthly father for his children. Our human affection, therefore, in its purest forms, is of the same kind as the Love of GOD Himself, it is not of the earth earthy. Much more will easily suggest itself in this connection, I will therefore leave the matter here.

The second also of these Higher Space capacities which I have mentioned, viz. Faith, in like manner finds our bounds too strait; it is indeed the foundation of our relations with one another, but it too has the capacity for embracing the Highest, therefore of reaching Him. Faith is not earth-born, it is another attribute of our Bodies of Extension.

And Hope, the faculty of which we are told distinctly that it entereth into that within the veil, cannot find range enough in our Space for its full exercise.

L

These then are faculties or senses which, while to some limited extent they manifest themselves in our Low Space, are not belonging to it, nor, speaking accurately, to our physical bodies in any sense. They cannot find full scope for exercise within our limits in this world, nor can they be satisfied with what they find in it; they reach out beyond our Space into regions which otherwise we cannot enter, bearing us into a consciousness of what we cannot see, and assuring us of what would otherwise remain unknown.

They reveal to us, each in its own way, what but for them would still be hidden; and thus it appears that though at present these Higher Senses are weighed down by our connection with our bodily encumbrances, still they have expression in the Higher Space, with members suited to that expression likewise in the Higher Space.

As yet they are only in the early stages of development, because they are not wholly free from the imperfections and infirmities which their association with our mortal bodies has forced upon them ; but when the time shall come for us to be set free from the burden of the flesh, there will be opportunities for their expansion, and growth proportional to the Greater Freedom which shall be granted to us.

With these three there should, no doubt, be numbered many more of our higher aptitudes and capabilities, the which, though exercised upon materials which are of earth, for want of others, are yet not wholly earth-born. These, we may conjecture, will find facilities more fitting for their employment when we have left this world behind.

But conjecture, pure and simple, however interesting, is not now to be pursued ; we will pass on to more solid ground.

XIX

CONCERNING THE KENOSIS, AND THE EARTH-LIFE OF OUR LORD

Let us now turn to the consideration of our Lord's Life on earth, especially the earlier part of it.

From our point of view, that is, having our theory in mind, we have to think of Him before His Incarnation as dwelling in the Highest Space of all, in the Bosom of the Father; from thence He came to Earth, taking to Himself our human nature.

We will try to obtain independently a description of what we should expect to be the case if one from Higher Space should come into our world. If this agrees with what is written of Him, then so far the theory is justified.

It has already been seen that as we contemplate in ascending succession the series of Higher Spaces, the limitations of each Lower Space in order pass away in the next Higher Space, until in the Highest Space of all, all limitations of whatever kind are gone.

For the solution of our problem we shall have to reverse this succession.

In order that we may be sure of our ground we will first consider the simplest case, and discuss a hypothetical descent from Space of Four Directions into our own Space. This is only to reverse the process which we went through when we were speaking of the condition of the Departed.

A person so descending would lose much of freedom, and would find himself in a much worse condition than that which he occupied before. All would seem strange to him. Retaining the memory of what he had left behind, he would find all his new surroundings terribly cramped. Having been accustomed to the Greater Freedom, he would not, like us, accept his new surroundings as inevitable, but knowing the better would miss it sorely. Habituated to free extension in Four Directions, he would feel grievously hampered and imprisoned in only Three; acquainted with free Space, he would feel himself almost unendurably shut in within the limits of what he had regarded as a film.

This gives us an idea of some sort as to the method to be followed in solving our problem. But we will try to get another and more vivid illustration which shall be more within our own experience, or at least more under our own eyes.

If by an effort of imagination we could regard ourselves as being compelled to live and move in a narrow passage between two high walls, beyond which nothing could reach us, even this would not adequately describe to us the loss of freedom which would be experienced by one who came to dwell with us from Space of Four Directions. In order to obtain anything like a sufficient conception of his experience it would be necessary to bring those walls quite close together, till the space between them became of infinitesimal width, till in fact we were shut up in Space of Two Directions, and retaining our consciousness of powers which we could not exercise, were compelled to pass our time incarcerated in this absolutely narrow Space.

It is an interesting exercise to endeavour to realise what such conditions of existence would represent to us, and to try to constitute the life programme of beings in such a state. But it would be beyond my present purpose, which is only to suggest a means of realising what would be the experience of one coming down to us from the next Higher Space. Thus much is evident, that he would lose the Greater Freedom which was his.

Now in our Lord's case we have to deal not only with a descent from Space of

Four Directions, but from the Highest Space of all.

Though this is not an accurate way of putting it, we shall find it convenient to think of Him, when coming to dwell with man, as renouncing in turn the special privileges of each Higher Region, and accepting in turn the successive limitations of each successive Lower Space, till, reaching our Space, the last renunciation would be made, and the last restriction accepted in the narrow limits of our world.

It is of course only generally that we can speak of this, but the impression left upon our minds is evidently of this kind, that, coming in such a way, and submitting Himself to our conditions and our surroundings, He gave up a position in which there were absolutely no restrictions, and became subject to very narrow bounds, in which His Essential powers were confined and circumscribed.

But this is not all. Not only did He come to Earth, but He became a Son of

Man. He took our nature upon Him in the womb of the Blessed Virgin, of her substance. So that it was not only the conditions of our Space that He accepted but also the conditions of our life. There is, of course, a great distinction between the two.

Entering upon our life, He did not take it in its mature development, but began it as we begin it in His mother's womb. Thus intimating that He had condescended to submit Himself to all the necessary infirmities of our life.

This clears the way for the attempt to describe what is to be expected, from our point of view, to be the course of His life.

Born as an infant, we should expect to find Him like other infants, subject to all the necessary conditions of infant life, its ignorance, its weakness, its unconsciousness of future development, its happy simplicity. We should not expect to find Him a prodigy, but a purely typical child, with all the peculiarly winning charm with which all true children are invested perhaps more marked than in any other, since that charm is derived from the power which infants have of shewing two characteristics of Higher Space, Trustfulness and Love, the which with Him, Whose origin was the Highest Space of all, were even more natural than in the case of any other child. We should also expect that the innocence of childhood would in His case be more noticeable than in the case of any other infant.

In the infant stage of man's life, whatever capacities, whatever faculties belong to the individual, time is needed before the body or the mind is able to express them. All powers have to train or mould or form their agent before they can be exhibited. Speaking in a general way, the greater are the powers latent within the child, the longer is this stage or period of formation.

We should therefore expect that the early years of our Lord would be marked not by any precocious signs of what should be, but by a trustful and loving simplicity, in which by reason of the perfection of His exalted Nature, He would shew a pure and holy character, such as that of Adam in the days of his innocency, since sin is not a necessary infirmity of man.

During this holy Childhood, while the Higher Faculties, both those which He had in common with other children and those which belonged to Himself Alone, were gradually accommodating their surroundings to themselves, and themselves to their surroundings, some faint perception, such as are granted to gifted children, and incline them to one form of active life rather than another, would begin to dawn on Him, and as time passed would become more clear, till He would recognise that He was set apart from others for a special work.

Not all at once would this consciousness deepen into definite conviction ; for, as we have seen, time is required for the human agent or instrument to become adapted to the comprehension and the service of the

Higher Faculties; or, in other words, for the Faculties of Higher Space to train the lower parts of our nature so as to be able to express themselves through them. But we should expect that the day would come when the habitual study of the Scriptures, enjoined on every Jewish boy, and the constant conversation which went on around Him concerning the Law and the Prophets, which spoke of Him, would gradually lead Him to recognise Himself described in the Prophetical Books, and so to recognise His Mission.

Yet after this knowledge had been gained in its earliest and most elementary form, His powers would require longer time for growth before they attained their full development, or, more accurately speaking, before they could complete the education of their human agent. For indeed the very greatness of those powers would render this more difficult, as the cramping force of the surroundings of our Lower Space would be more felt in proportion to the greatness of the capacities which struggled in it for their manifestation.

The time would come at last when the powers of Higher Space would have become, so to speak, acclimatised, and when the human body would be fitted for their use. And then we should expect to find that in Him would be exhibited not only the use of these powers at His will, but also the most acute, the Highest susceptibilities, the most perfect love, the truest, tenderest sympathy, in Him most natural,—and because most natural, most perfect,—because of His perfect insight and penetration.

Mighty Works, the employment of His power in obedience to His sympathy and love, would be of course; and mighty words, such as would sway the hearts of multitudes, would accompany them.

But yet since both were prompted by a nature far above the nature of mankind, we should expect to find that in the case of many who saw and heard, the effect would be but transient. Such as had not received the training of their Higher aptitudes would not be able to grasp what was so far above them, nor in a moment to learn what it had cost Him many long years to understand. And more, that they would be the last to recognise and acknowledge Him, who definitely declined a standard higher than their own.

Not only would the effect of His teaching on them be transient, but, further, the strain to which it called them would raise feelings of jealousy in some of them, of fierce resentment in others, till He, far in advance of His own age, would share with others, who have been pioneers of progress, a martyrdom at the hands of exasperated would-be rivals.

All this agrees so perfectly with what we know of the life of Jesus that I have hesitated as to whether it should be allowed to stand. But since, so far as my consciousness is concerned, I have simply set down what has been suggested by our theory, I have not cut it out ; for even if the force of an independent construction be denied to it, still it may be felt that as an explanation of some difficulties concerning our Lord's life on Earth, and especially of the Kenosis, it gives a broad and not unreasonable account of them from the point on which we stand, and also affords a reason for what we have observed or learnt in the narrative of that Life which we possess.

We will pursue the enquiry farther. It seems to me that the foregoing description of our Lord's descent from the Highest Space, and His renunciation of the freedom of that Space, with all that is signified by that freedom, answers exactly to S. Paul's phrase, "He emptied Himself of His glory," and gives an intelligible account of what it means.

And again, that His own expression, that He was "straitened" till the hour of His death should come, receives a complete and most remarkable elucidation under the description of His acceptance of the restrictions of Lower Space.

And yet again, that this acceptance of our disabilities is described most naturally in these words, "Though He was rich, for our sakes He became poor."

Our theory, moreover, explains what some at least have found it very difficult to understand about His growth in Childhood, and His ignorance as to Who and What He was, until that day in the Temple when He learnt for the first time clearly from whence He came and Who His Father was.

It tells us too, comprehensibly, how for a time He was lower than the Angels, since for a time He dwelt in a Lower Space than they.

Some light is also thrown upon the mystery of the Temptation in the Wilderness, in which the words "If Thou be the Son of GOD" at least suggest that the Devil did not know that He was truly such.

For, recalling the fact that to pass from the Highest Space to ours there is no need to traverse any intermediate Space, the descent from the Bosom of the Father would have taken place in a region to which the Devil had no access; he therefore could not be cognisant of it, nor could he absolutely know Who it was that he addressed. The Voice from Heaven he would have heard, proclaiming, " This is My beloved Son," the descent of the Holy Ghost he would have seen, the purity of the perfect Childhood must have been a constant source of wonderment to him, but what was the meaning of these manifestations we may well suppose he did not recognise; something great no doubt, but how great as yet he did not know.

XX

CONCERNING THE RISEN BODY OF OUR LORD

Taking up the story of the Life after the Resurrection, we have what is an obvious understanding of the appearances and disappearances of our Lord.

For having died as man, as man the unseen path, the Fourth Direction, which leads to Higher Space, was opened to Him. He was as man enabled to see and use that path.

Taking again His Body, never to lay It aside again, He did not forfeit that which had been gained, but still retained the power of travelling along that path which is unseen by us. His Body, having entered and returned from the grave, was freed from all its imperfections, freed from the bonds which had confined It to our Space.

Thus there is no difficulty in perceiving how it was that at Emmaus He vanished out of the sight of the two Disciples. He simply passed along the unseen path into the Higher Space, where their eyes could not follow Him.

There is no reason or even justification for supposing anything about a so-called spiritual body, with powers of condensing itself at one time and at another of becoming etherealised; there is in truth no room for such a supposition. The Body was a real human body, tangible, solid, able to receive both meat and drink, and to such a body performances such as these are, so far as our experience of human bodies, by this time a somewhat long experience, entirely inconceivable.

So with regard to His appearance on the same evening, and on that day week; there is no call to speak of entering the room through a closed door, in virtue of an indefinable property with which His Risen Body has been conjecturally invested. He simply passed from that spot in the Higher Space which adjoined the spot in the room which He wished to occupy, and so coming from the Unseen, He stood in the midst of His Disciples, finding no obstacle of any kind before Him. And in like manner He departed from them.

XXI

CONCERNING THE ASCENSION OF OUR LORD

When the time came for the departure of the Lord from the Earth He did not leave His Disciples as at other times after His Resurrection, but in such a way as that it should be clear to them that His departure was definite, and that they should see Him no more among them as before. Therefore having taken them with Him to Mount Olivet, He rose from the Earth for a certain distance, not so far as to disappear gradually, but apparently only a short way, and then a cloud veiled Him from their sight, and under cover of the cloud He passed into the Higher Space, to appear on earth no more. While from the Higher

Space two " men " came forth, fulfilled their message to the Disciples, and departed as they had come, entering into the Higher Space again.

Before quitting this subject, we may note that the words of our Lord, " I am not yet ascended to My Father," become invested with a plain meaning. Though He had entered into the Higher Space, He had not yet ascended into the Highest Space, that return to where He was before had not then taken place. Up to this time this has been a difficulty to my mind at least, now that difficulty is removed.

XXII

CONCERNING OUR OWN GROWTH IN GRACE

The train of thought which has occupied us during this last discussion has its value in another way. It helps to explain how it is that our growth in grace is apparently so slow.

In order that we may advance in the way of holiness, it is essential that the Holy Spirit should make His abode in us.

Now we have seen that in the case of our Lord, when He, Divine, took to Himself the Manhood, even though the Godhead and the Manhood became one Person, time was needed for growth and development, for the moulding, forming, and adapting the lower elements of the Lower

Space to the requirements of the Higher elements, the higher members in the Higher Space, and this although with our nature He took only the necessary imperfections and infirmities of it.

In our case there is a very essential difference. We are by reason of our fallen nature subject to sin, our nature is spoilt by sin. The human and the Divine in our case are not so perfectly joined together as they were in His. With us there is much to be undone as well as much to be done before we can grow in grace as we desire. For this time is necessary. The lower elements must not only be trained by the Divine power, but they must also learn subjection. Not only must the higher faculties be matured, but the resistance of the lower and material elements must be overcome.

While then we pray for greater advancement and more rapid progress, we need not become impatient or disappointed by reason of the apparent slowness of the answer to our prayers; since the obstacles are very many, and the impediments very great in the way of our progress in the Higher Life.

To be advanced from glory to glory, that is, from Space to Space, is no light matter; indeed, it is a matter for deep thankfulness that such a thing is possible at all. That GOD should condescend to dwell with us and in us, amid such terribly unfavourable surroundings, and use His Power in our behalf with such never-failing patience, encouraging and advancing us from Space to Space, and ministering to our growth in each Space as we reach it, transforming us in this way into a nearer likeness to our Lord, this calls for gratitude, and not impatience, though since the work is so infinitely great, it necessarily seems to be slow in progress.

XXIII

SUMMARY

I now return to the general view of our subject, which I have treated with as much regard to brevity as was compatible with my desire to give a broad view of the most important points connected with it.

We began by stating as a proposition, that it is in Higher Space that we are to look for the key to the understanding of the Unseen. Then taking this as a working hypothesis, and assuming that the Higher Space exists not only in imagination, but as an actual reality, we proceeded to consider on this basis a variety of what are commonly called "spiritual" subjects.

These, we have seen, may be treated

from an almost physical point of view, and that intelligibly.

On this hypothesis we have been able to see how the future life and the present life are in close connection with each other, how a real continuity exists between them. The other life being no pale reflection of our present life; the other world no misty cloudland, peopled by shadows which are only vaguely to be regarded as enjoying happiness in a negative, and to us unsatisfying sense. We have seen something at all events of conditions which are real to our understanding, and most desirable to our minds, surpassing in every respect the very best that earth can give.

We have learnt that the Unseen is not invisible, but only out of sight; and that, not owing to an immensity of distance, but because of the necessary relations between our Space and Higher Space.

We have found that our hypothesis, with the principles that flow directly from it, has not only spoken to us of the state of the Departed, but has also given us a definition of the words "spirit" and "spiritual" which has dispelled the mist by which so many of the most beautiful ideas connected with our Higher Nature have been obscured; and in doing so has shewn us what is almost a physical truth concerning our souls, our Spirits, and their relation in the communion of Saints with those who have gone before.

With humble reverence approaching the thought of GOD Himself, we have been able to learn something intelligible about His Nature, His Being, and His attributes, for we have found a clue to the comprehension of the manner of His Omnipotence, His Omniscience, His Omnipresence.

We have seen how in this light the Life of our Lord Jesus Christ has become clearer to our understanding, and the same argument has yielded results concerning the work of the Holy Spirit in our hearts.

The mystery of the appearances and

disappearances of our Lord is seen to be most plain; and not only so but at the same time we are able to see how in accordance with His promise He, though unseen, is present with us and in the midst of us when we are met together in His Name.

The ministry of the Angels has become plain to our apprehension, for we have found how they, unseen, may yet assist us and bear us in their hands. And many other thoughts of a like nature have suggested themselves.

Many passages have been quoted from the Bible, many more might easily have been quoted which may be fairly claimed as supporting our contention. While, perhaps, a more important point, I have not found any places which are in opposition to it.

This summary deals with a considerable number of subjects which are seen to be susceptible of treatment from one single point of view; it shews them not as isolated phenomena, but as belonging to one group; and it may be claimed for a theory which combines so many diverse points, that it is worthy of consideration.

It is true that all depends on what is admittedly an unknown direction. But this is not to be wondered at, nor is the theory to be rejected on this account. For it is the Unknown that we have been studying. And at least this must be acknowledged, that when the one unknown is simply the direction of a line, of which mathematical science can tell us much, a line which has actually been visualised by some persons, we have been brought from a situation of very great and even absolute complexity into a position of comparative simplicity.

XXIV

A GENEALOGY OF THE THEORY

THERE is another consideration of an entirely different kind which appears to me to be of interest in this investigation. I am aware that in the case of many others it will not be regarded as adding any weight to the preceding, but for all that I will produce it. It is this, that the conception which has been discussed is not by any means a new one, but on the contrary a very old one indeed.

Without pretending to an intimate acquaintance with the doctrines of those whom I shall quote, it still is possible to say that one can recognise in them the fact that under one form or other our theory has been held continuously for many ages.

It has appeared in many different disguises, and it would seem in many cases at least to have been held by the majority in ignorance of the manner of its truth.

Be this as it may, the first principle of our theory is to be traced in many systems of religion and philosophy, viz. that outside the limits of our Space there are other Spaces beyond the reach of our ordinary experience, and that these Spaces are inhabited.

We will trace this genealogy backwards. Beginning with the present day, Theosophists teach that there are seven planes of existence, seven aspects of a man's nature. Some of these parts of his nature may be and generally are latent, but by the use of proper means he may be educated till they become manifest in various forms of activity. And apparently on the Higher Planes, or some of them, a man may be in communication with higher natures than those of earth.

This strongly resembles what has been

said above as to our Bodies of Extension in the Higher Space, and this is what constitutes the special interest of their teaching on this point.

It is not necessary to follow their doctrine farther, but we may note that they claim, and have the right to claim, the weight of ancient tradition in favour of their teaching, for they declare that they have received it from a far antiquity, from the old students of hidden things—the Magi and the Astrologers.

The Spiritists speak of circles in the other world, inhabited by spirits of various grades and various powers, these spirits being either those of the Departed, or of Angelic or Diabolic nature.

That Spiritists claim to be able to control these spirits or some of them is not now to our purpose. I simply quote their doctrine because, apart from the use they make of it, it agrees with what has been said above, as to the Higher Spaces and their inhabitants.

Spiritists do not claim that they have invented or discovered this truth, but state, and are right in stating, that they have inherited it from older ages.

Going farther back in point of time, we find the same kind of belief among occultists of all sorts, and they inherited it from their teachers.

This belief must have been very strong indeed, and its attractions must have been very great. For in the Dark Ages it was held by very many in spite of the ban of the Church under which all who dared to profess it lay, in spite too of the dangers by which its adherents were threatened both from the religious and the civil powers.

In spite of all these dangers the truth survived; and perhaps more wonderful still, it survived in spite of the errors which gathered round it, in spite too of the discredit which was transferred to it from those who, holding it in error, associated it with magic and sorcery.

Again, going farther back, we find that the Gnostics, still holding the truth in error, taught it in a form which apparently was purer than that adopted by their successors.

They spoke of Æons of different degrees, dwelling in heavens of higher or lower rank, which step by step led their thoughts upwards towards the Pleroma, where, as they taught, GOD dwells in unapproachable light. The truth was there, however much disguised, however little understood, however grievously admixed with error.

The Gnostics did not claim that they had found out this truth. They adopted and adapted it from yet earlier systems of magic and philosophy, interweaving with what they drew from them some points which they derived from Christianity.

Thus then we have an almost if not quite unbroken chain of tradition, carrying us back to very early times. And it does not call for any very large amount of imagination if we venture to trace the belief even farther back through the magicians and sorcerers of the East, the Persians and Chaldæans, probably the successors of Balaam, who, as we know, lived towards the end of his life in the East, though at an earlier period, if we may believe the Jewish legends, he was associated, as their chief, with the magicians of Ancient Egypt, men who, according to the testimony of the Sacred records, were certainly adepts in strange accomplishments.

It seems almost incredible that at this very early period of history men should be able to discover a truth like this. Far more incredible than that it was handed down from a far earlier time.

The suggestion seems to be this, that Shem, who is described in Jewish records as a man of great piety and learning, received the knowledge of it before the Flood, and that it was a relic of the knowledge of Adam himself, from whom, by only two transmissions, Shem could have received it. If this were so, it is easy to see how from him it would spread, and like the religion which he taught to his descendants, become deteriorated as time went on.

But however this may be, and of course the last steps are almost pure conjecture, the fact remains that we can find something very like the doctrine of Higher Space very far back in ancient history.

Another part of our theory also receives the support of Antiquity in the same way and through the same channels, viz. that which speaks of our members in the Higher Space, our Bodies of Extension.

It will be evident that I am speaking of what is called the "Astral body" of which occultists of whatever denomination tell us. In this case we may omit the intervening stages, and recognise in the old records of the Egyptians the same belief in another form. They taught that in what we know as "soul" there are seven constituents, with different properties. This is their method of describing what we have called Bodies of Extension in the Higher Space.

As regards the theory itself there is no lack of support in what are often called superstitions, but may more truly be recognised as debased beliefs.

Such are the legends of incubi and succubi, and the phenomena known as cases of obsession, which point to interference with the spiritual side of man by beings not belonging to our Space; the which we find authenticated in both the Old and New Testaments whenever we read of the possession of men by evil spirits.

Without going into details, it is enough to add to this that all the bewildering array of spells and incantations of every kind, wherever met with, are suggestions that man has a spiritual side on which he may be reached by unseen agencies that are under the control of those who know how to compel their services.

To this may also possibly be referred

the powers of hypnotism, mesmerism, and the like.

Once more, I will allude to the Moslem belief in a plurality of heavens, which are described in the most realistic terms, and seem to find countenance in what S. Paul says about his experiences in the Third Heaven, to which he tells us he was caught up, whether in the body or out of the body he could not tell, where he saw things that could not be described by the tongue of man, since the speech of Lower Space cannot put into words what passes in the Higher Space.

The Indian belief in the existence of many orders of heavens and hells may also be quoted.

Many more witnesses might easily be called who would speak in language which our theory enables us to understand upon this subject, but the above may suffice for my present purpose, which is to shew that amid much error, much ignorance, much superstition the truth has been preserved by its own vitality, the which if it were not so powerful must have been crushed out by the hands through which it has passed.

Not only has it not been crushed out, but on the contrary it has given something of its own life to the systems which have received it, however much disguised, under however grotesque forms, in East and West alike; and it may be fairly conjectured that it is in virtue of this life that the Non-Christian religions of the world maintain their wonderful ascendency, in a way that would not only be surprising but impossible unless they had some salt of truth to preserve them and their beliefs.

THE END

Printed by R. & R. CLARK, *Edinburgh.*

January 1893

A Catalogue

of

Theological Works

published by

Macmillan & Co.

Bedford Street, Strand, London

CONTENTS

	PAGE
THE BIBLE:—	
History of the Bible	1
Biblical History	1
The Old Testament	1
The New Testament	3
HISTORY OF THE CHRISTIAN CHURCH	6
THE CHURCH OF ENGLAND	6
DEVOTIONAL BOOKS	8
THE FATHERS	8
HYMNOLOGY	9
SERMONS, LECTURES, ADDRESSES, AND THEOLOGICAL ESSAYS	9

January 1893.

MACMILLAN AND CO.'S THEOLOGICAL CATALOGUE

The Bible

HISTORY OF THE BIBLE

THE ENGLISH BIBLE: An External and Critical History of the various English Translations of Scripture. By Prof. JOHN EADIE. 2 vols. 8vo. 28s.

THE BIBLE IN THE CHURCH. By Right Rev. Bishop WESTCOTT. 10th Edition. 18mo. 4s. 6d.

BIBLICAL HISTORY

BIBLE LESSONS. By Rev. E. A. ABBOTT. Crown 8vo. 4s. 6d.

SIDE-LIGHTS UPON BIBLE HISTORY. By Mrs. SYDNEY BUXTON. Illustrated. Crown 8vo. 5s.

STORIES FROM THE BIBLE. By Rev. A. J. CHURCH. Illustrated. Two Series. Crown 8vo. 3s. 6d. each.

BIBLE READINGS SELECTED FROM THE PENTATEUCH AND THE BOOK OF JOSHUA. By Rev. J. A. CROSS. 2nd Edition. Globe 8vo. 2s. 6d.

CHILDREN'S TREASURY OF BIBLE STORIES. By Mrs. H. GASKOIN. 18mo. 1s. each. Part I. Old Testament; II. New Testament; III. Three Apostles.

A CLASS-BOOK OF OLD TESTAMENT HISTORY. By Rev. Canon MACLEAR. With Four Maps. 18mo. 4s. 6d.

A CLASS-BOOK OF NEW TESTAMENT HISTORY. Including the connection of the Old and New Testament. By the same. 18mo. 5s. 6d.

A SHILLING BOOK OF OLD TESTAMENT HISTORY. By the same. 18mo. 1s.

A SHILLING BOOK OF NEW TESTAMENT HISTORY. By the same. 18mo. 1s.

THE OLD TESTAMENT

SCRIPTURE READINGS FOR SCHOOLS AND FAMILIES. By C. M. YONGE. Globe 8vo. 1s. 6d. each; also with comments, 3s. 6d. each.—First Series: GENESIS TO DEUTERONOMY.—Second Series: JOSHUA TO SOLOMON.—Third Series: KINGS AND THE PROPHETS.—Fourth Series: THE GOSPEL TIMES.—Fifth Series; APOSTOLIC TIMES.

The Old Testament—*continued.*

WARBURTONIAN LECTURES ON THE MINOR PROPHETS. By Rev. A. F. KIRKPATRICK, B.D. Crown 8vo. [*In the Press.*

THE PATRIARCHS AND LAWGIVERS OF THE OLD TESTAMENT. By FREDERICK DENISON MAURICE. New Edition. Crown 8vo. 3s. 6d.

THE PROPHETS AND KINGS OF THE OLD TESTAMENT. By the same. New Edition. Crown 8vo. 3s. 6d.

THE CANON OF THE OLD TESTAMENT. An Essay on the Growth and Formation of the Hebrew Canon of Scripture. By Rev. Prof. H. E. RYLE. Crown 8vo. 6s.

THE EARLY NARRATIVES OF GENESIS. By Rev. Prof. H. E. RYLE. Cr. 8vo. 3s. net.

The Pentateuch—

AN HISTORICO-CRITICAL INQUIRY INTO THE ORIGIN AND COMPOSITION OF THE HEXATEUCH (PENTATEUCH AND BOOK OF JOSHUA). By Prof. A. KUENEN. Translated by PHILIP H. WICKSTEED, M.A. 8vo. 14s.

The Psalms—

THE PSALMS CHRONOLOGICALLY ARRANGED. An Amended Version, with Historical Introductions and Explanatory Notes. By Four Friends. New Edition. Crown 8vo. 5s. net.

GOLDEN TREASURY PSALTER. The Student's Edition. Being an Edition with briefer Notes of "The Psalms Chronologically Arranged by Four Friends." 18mo. 3s. 6d.

THE PSALMS. With Introductions and Critical Notes. By A. C. JENNINGS, M.A., and W. H. LOWE, M.A. In 2 vols. 2nd Edition. Crown 8vo. 10s. 6d. each.

INTRODUCTION TO THE STUDY AND USE OF THE PSALMS. By Rev. J. F. THRUPP. 2nd Edition. 2 vols. 8vo. 21s.

Isaiah—

ISAIAH XL.—LXVI. With the Shorter Prophecies allied to it. By MATTHEW ARNOLD. With Notes. Crown 8vo. 5s.

ISAIAH OF JERUSALEM. In the Authorised English Version, with Introduction, Corrections, and Notes. By the same. Cr. 8vo. 4s. 6d.

A BIBLE-READING FOR SCHOOLS. The Great Prophecy of Israel's Restoration (Isaiah xl.-lxvi.) Arranged and Edited for Young Learners. By the same. 4th Edition. 18mo. 1s.

COMMENTARY ON THE BOOK OF ISAIAH, Critical, Historical, and Prophetical; including a Revised English Translation. By T. R. BIRKS. 2nd Edition. 8vo. 12s. 6d.

THE BOOK OF ISAIAH CHRONOLOGICALLY ARRANGED. By T. K. CHEYNE. Crown 8vo. 7s. 6d.

Zechariah—

THE HEBREW STUDENT'S COMMENTARY ON ZECHARIAH, Hebrew and LXX. By W. H. LOWE, M.A. 8vo. 10s. 6d.

THE NEW TESTAMENT

APOCRYPHAL GOSPEL OF PETER. The Greek Text of the Newly-Discovered Fragment. 8vo. Sewed. 1s.

THE NEW TESTAMENT. Essay on the Right Estimation of MS. Evidence in the Text of the New Testament. By T. R. BIRKS. Crown 8vo. 3s. 6d.

THE SOTERIOLOGY OF THE NEW TESTAMENT. By W. P. DU BOSE, M.A. Crown 8vo. 7s. 6d.

THE MESSAGES OF THE BOOKS. Being Discourses and Notes on the Books of the New Testament. By Ven. Archdeacon FARRAR. 8vo. 14s.

THE CLASSICAL ELEMENT IN THE NEW TESTAMENT. Considered as a Proof of its Genuineness, with an Appendix on the Oldest Authorities used in the Formation of the Canon. By C. H. HOOLE. 8vo. 10s. 6d.

ON A FRESH REVISION OF THE ENGLISH NEW TESTAMENT. With an Appendix on the last Petition of the Lord's Prayer. By Bishop LIGHTFOOT. Crown 8vo. 7s. 6d.

DISSERTATIONS ON THE APOSTOLIC AGE. By Bishop LIGHTFOOT. 8vo. 14s.

THE UNITY OF THE NEW TESTAMENT. By F. D. MAURICE. 2nd Edition. 2 vols. Crown 8vo. 12s.

A COMPANION TO THE GREEK TESTAMENT AND THE ENGLISH VERSION. By PHILIP SCHAFF, D.D. Cr. 8vo. 12s.

A GENERAL SURVEY OF THE HISTORY OF THE CANON OF THE NEW TESTAMENT DURING THE FIRST FOUR CENTURIES. By Right Rev. Bishop WESTCOTT. 6th Edition. Crown 8vo. 10s. 6d.

THE NEW TESTAMENT IN THE ORIGINAL GREEK. The Text revised by Bishop WESTCOTT, D.D., and Prof. F. J. A. HORT, D.D. 2 vols. Crown 8vo. 10s. 6d. each.—Vol. I. Text; II. Introduction and Appendix.

THE NEW TESTAMENT IN THE ORIGINAL GREEK, for Schools. The Text revised by Bishop WESTCOTT, D.D., and F. J. A. HORT, D.D. 12mo, cloth, 4s. 6d.; 18mo, roan, red edges, 5s. 6d.; morocco, gilt edges, 6s. 6d.

THE GOSPELS—

THE COMMON TRADITION OF THE SYNOPTIC GOSPELS, in the Text of the Revised Version. By Rev. E. A. ABBOTT and W. G. RUSHBROOKE. Crown 8vo. 3s. 6d.

SYNOPTICON: An Exposition of the Common Matter of the Synoptic Gospels. By W. G. RUSHBROOKE. Printed in Colours. In Six Parts, and Appendix. 4to.—Part I. 3s. 6d. Parts II. and III. 7s. Parts IV. V. and VI. with Indices, 10s. 6d. Appendices, 10s. 6d. Complete in 1 vol., 35s. Indispensable to a Theological Student.

INTRODUCTION TO THE STUDY OF THE FOUR GOSPELS. By Right Rev. Bishop WESTCOTT. 7th Ed. Cr. 8vo. 10s. 6d.

THE COMPOSITION OF THE FOUR GOSPELS. By Rev. ARTHUR WRIGHT. Crown 8vo. 5s.

Gospel of St. Matthew—
> THE GOSPEL ACCORDING TO ST. MATTHEW. Greek Text as Revised by Bishop WESTCOTT and Dr. HORT. With Introduction and Notes by Rev. A. SLOMAN, M.A. Fcap. 8vo. 2s. 6d.
> CHOICE NOTES ON ST. MATTHEW, drawn from Old and New Sources. Crown 8vo. 4s. 6d. (St. Matthew and St. Mark in 1 vol. 9s.)

Gospel of St. Mark—
> SCHOOL READINGS IN THE GREEK TESTAMENT. Being the Outlines of the Life of our Lord as given by St. Mark, with additions from the Text of the other Evangelists. Edited, with Notes and Vocabulary, by Rev. A. CALVERT, M.A. Fcap. 8vo. 2s. 6d.
> CHOICE NOTES ON ST. MARK, drawn from Old and New Sources. Cr. 8vo. 4s. 6d. (St. Matthew and St. Mark in 1 vol. 9s.)

Gospel of St. Luke—
> THE GOSPEL ACCORDING TO ST. LUKE. The Greek Text as Revised by Bishop WESTCOTT and Dr. HORT. With Introduction and Notes by Rev. J. BOND, M.A. Fcap. 8vo. 2s. 6d.
> CHOICE NOTES ON ST. LUKE, drawn from Old and New Sources. Crown 8vo. 4s. 6d.
> THE GOSPEL OF THE KINGDOM OF HEAVEN. A Course of Lectures on the Gospel of St. Luke. By F. D. MAURICE. 3rd Edition. Crown 8vo. 6s.

Gospel of St. John—
> THE CENTRAL TEACHING OF CHRIST. Being a Study and Exposition of St. John, Chapters XIII. to XVII. By Rev. CANON BERNARD, M.A. Crown 8vo. 7s. 6d.
> THE GOSPEL OF ST. JOHN. By F. D. MAURICE. 8th Ed. Cr. 8vo. 6s.
> CHOICE NOTES ON ST. JOHN, drawn from Old and New Sources. Crown 8vo. 4s. 6d.

THE ACTS OF THE APOSTLES—
> THE ACTS OF THE APOSTLES. Being the Greek Text as Revised by Bishop WESTCOTT and Dr. HORT. With Explanatory Notes by T. E. PAGE, M.A. Fcap. 8vo. 3s. 6d.
> THE CHURCH OF THE FIRST DAYS. THE CHURCH OF JERUSALEM. THE CHURCH OF THE GENTILES. THE CHURCH OF THE WORLD. Lectures on the Acts of the Apostles. By Very Rev. C. J. VAUGHAN. Crown 8vo. 10s. 6d.

THE EPISTLES of St. Paul—
> ST. PAUL'S EPISTLE TO THE ROMANS. The Greek Text, with English Notes. By Very Rev. C. J. VAUGHAN. 7th Edition. Crown 8vo. 7s. 6d.
> A COMMENTARY ON ST. PAUL'S TWO EPISTLES TO THE CORINTHIANS. Greek Text, with Commentary. By Rev. W. KAY. 8vo. 9s.

Of St. Paul—*continued.*
- ST. PAUL'S EPISTLE TO THE GALATIANS. A Revised Text, with Introduction, Notes, and Dissertations. By Bishop LIGHTFOOT. 10th Edition. 8vo. 12s.
- ST. PAUL'S EPISTLE TO THE PHILIPPIANS. A Revised Text, with Introduction, Notes, and Dissertations. By the same. 9th Edition. 8vo. 12s.
- ST. PAUL'S EPISTLE TO THE PHILIPPIANS. With translation, Paraphrase, and Notes for English Readers. By Very Rev. C. J. VAUGHAN. Crown 8vo. 5s.
- ST. PAUL'S EPISTLES TO THE COLOSSIANS AND TO PHILEMON. A Revised Text, with Introductions, etc. By Bishop LIGHTFOOT. 9th Edition. 8vo. 12s.
- THE EPISTLES OF ST. PAUL TO THE EPHESIANS, THE COLOSSIANS, AND PHILEMON. With Introductions and Notes. By Rev. J. LL. DAVIES. 2nd Edition. 8vo. 7s. 6d.
- THE EPISTLES OF ST. PAUL. For English Readers. Part I. containing the First Epistle to the Thessalonians. By Very Rev. C. J. VAUGHAN. 2nd Edition. 8vo. Sewed. 1s. 6d.
- ST. PAUL'S EPISTLES TO THE THESSALONIANS, COMMENTARY ON THE GREEK TEXT. By Prof. JOHN EADIE. 8vo. 12s.

The Epistle of St. James—
- THE EPISTLE OF ST. JAMES. The Greek Text, with Introduction and Notes. By Rev. JOSEPH MAYOR, M.A. 8vo. 14s.

The Epistles of St. John—
- THE EPISTLES OF ST. JOHN. By F. D. MAURICE. 4th Edition. Crown 8vo. 6s.
- THE EPISTLES OF ST. JOHN. The Greek Text, with Notes. By Right Rev. Bishop WESTCOTT. 3rd Edition. 8vo. 12s. 6d.

The Epistle to the Hebrews—
- THE EPISTLE TO THE HEBREWS IN GREEK AND ENGLISH. With Notes. By Rev. FREDERIC RENDALL. Crown 8vo. 6s.
- THE EPISTLE TO THE HEBREWS. English Text, with Commentary. By the same. Crown 8vo. 7s. 6d.
- THE EPISTLE TO THE HEBREWS. With Notes. By Very Rev. C. J. VAUGHAN. Crown 8vo. 7s. 6d.
- THE EPISTLE TO THE HEBREWS. The Greek Text, with Notes and Essays. By Right Rev. Bishop WESTCOTT. 8vo. 14s.

REVELATION—
- LECTURES ON THE APOCALYPSE. By F. D. MAURICE. 2nd Edition. Crown 8vo. 6s.
- LECTURES ON THE APOCALYPSE. By Rev. Prof. W. MILLIGAN. Crown 8vo. 5s.
- THE REVELATION OF ST. JOHN. By Rev. Prof. W. MILLIGAN. 2nd Edition. Crown 8vo. 7s. 6d.

REVELATION—*continued.*
  LECTURES ON THE REVELATION OF ST. JOHN. By Very
  Rev. C. J. VAUGHAN. 5th Edition. Crown 8vo. 10s. 6d.

  THE BIBLE WORD-BOOK. By W. ALDIS WRIGHT. 2nd Edition.
  Crown 8vo. 7s. 6d.

Christian Church, History of the

Church (Dean).—THE OXFORD MOVEMENT. Twelve Years, 1833-45. Globe 8vo. 5s.

Cunningham (Rev. John).—THE GROWTH OF THE CHURCH IN ITS ORGANISATION AND INSTITUTIONS. 8vo. 9s.

Dale (A. W. W.)—THE SYNOD OF ELVIRA, AND CHRISTIAN LIFE IN THE FOURTH CENTURY. Cr. 8vo. 10s. 6d.

Hardwick (Archdeacon).—A HISTORY OF THE CHRISTIAN CHURCH. Middle Age. Ed. by Bishop STUBBS. Cr. 8vo. 10s. 6d.
  A HISTORY OF THE CHRISTIAN CHURCH DURING THE REFORMATION. Revised by Bishop STUBBS. Cr. 8vo. 10s. 6d.

Hort (Dr. F. J. A.)—TWO DISSERTATIONS. I. On ΜΟΝΟΓΕΝΗΣ ΘΕΟΣ in Scripture and Tradition. II. On the "Constantinopolitan" Creed and other Eastern Creeds of the Fourth Century. 8vo. 7s. 6d.

Killen (W. D.)—ECCLESIASTICAL HISTORY OF IRELAND, FROM THE EARLIEST DATE TO THE PRESENT TIME. 2 vols. 8vo. 25s.

Simpson (W.)—AN EPITOME OF THE HISTORY OF THE CHRISTIAN CHURCH. Fcap. 8vo. 3s. 6d.

Vaughan (Very Rev. C. J., Dean of Llandaff).—THE CHURCH OF THE FIRST DAYS. THE CHURCH OF JERUSALEM. THE CHURCH OF THE GENTILES. THE CHURCH OF THE WORLD. Crown 8vo. 10s. 6d.

Ward (W.)—WILLIAM GEORGE WARD AND THE OXFORD MOVEMENT. Portrait. 8vo. 14s.

The Church of England

Catechism of—
  A CLASS-BOOK OF THE CATECHISM OF THE CHURCH OF ENGLAND. By Rev. Canon MACLEAR. 18mo. 1s. 6d.
  A FIRST CLASS-BOOK OF THE CATECHISM OF THE CHURCH OF ENGLAND, with Scripture Proofs for Junior Classes and Schools. By the same. 18mo. 6d.
  THE ORDER OF CONFIRMATION, with Prayers and Devotions. By the Rev. Canon MACLEAR. 32mo. 6d.

Collects—
COLLECTS OF THE CHURCH OF ENGLAND. With a Coloured Floral Design to each Collect. Crown 8vo. 12s.

Disestablishment—
DISESTABLISHMENT AND DISENDOWMENT. What are they? By Prof. E. A. FREEMAN. 4th Edition. Crown 8vo. 1s.

DISESTABLISHMENT: or, A Defence of the Principle of a National Church. By GEORGE HARWOOD. 8vo. 12s.

A DEFENCE OF THE CHURCH OF ENGLAND AGAINST DISESTABLISHMENT. By ROUNDELL, EARL OF SELBORNE. Crown 8vo. 2s. 6d.

ANCIENT FACTS & FICTIONS CONCERNING CHURCHES AND TITHES. By the same. 2nd Edition. Crown 8vo. 7s. 6d.

Dissent in its Relation to—
DISSENT IN ITS RELATION TO THE CHURCH OF ENGLAND. By Rev. G. H. CURTEIS. Bampton Lectures for 1871. Crown 8vo. 7s. 6d.

Holy Communion—
THE COMMUNION SERVICE FROM THE BOOK OF COMMON PRAYER, with Select Readings from the Writings of the Rev. F. D. MAURICE. Edited by Bishop COLENSO. 6th Edition. 16mo. 2s. 6d.

BEFORE THE TABLE: An Inquiry, Historical and Theological, into the Meaning of the Consecration Rubric in the Communion Service of the Church of England. By Very Rev. J. S. HOWSON. 8vo. 7s. 6d.

FIRST COMMUNION, with Prayers and Devotions for the newly Confirmed. By Rev. Canon MACLEAR. 32mo. 6d.

A MANUAL OF INSTRUCTION FOR CONFIRMATION AND FIRST COMMUNION, with Prayers and Devotions. By the same. 32mo. 2s.

Liturgy—
A COMPANION TO THE LECTIONARY. By Rev. W. BENHAM, B.D. Crown 8vo. 4s. 6d.

AN INTRODUCTION TO THE CREEDS. By Rev. Canon MACLEAR. 18mo. 3s. 6d.

AN INTRODUCTION TO THE THIRTY-NINE ARTICLES. By the same. 18mo. [*In the Press.*

A HISTORY OF THE BOOK OF COMMON PRAYER. By Rev. F. PROCTER. 18th Edition. Crown 8vo. 10s. 6d.

AN ELEMENTARY INTRODUCTION TO THE BOOK OF COMMON PRAYER. By Rev. F. PROCTER and Rev. Canon MACLEAR. 18mo. 2s. 6d.

TWELVE DISCOURSES ON SUBJECTS CONNECTED WITH THE LITURGY AND WORSHIP OF THE CHURCH OF ENGLAND. By Very Rev. C. J. VAUGHAN. 4th Edition. Fcap. 8vo. 6s.

Devotional Books

Brooke (S. A.)—FORM OF MORNING AND EVENING PRAYER, and for the Administration of the Lord's Supper, together with the Baptismal and Marriage Services, Bedford Chapel, Bloomsbury. Fcap. 8vo. 1s. net.

Eastlake (Lady).—FELLOWSHIP: LETTERS ADDRESSED TO MY SISTER-MOURNERS. Crown 8vo. 2s. 6d.

IMITATIO CHRISTI, Libri IV. Printed in Borders after Holbein, Dürer, and other old Masters, containing Dances of Death, Acts of Mercy, Emblems, etc. Crown 8vo. 7s. 6d.

Kingsley (Charles).—OUT OF THE DEEP: WORDS FOR THE SORROWFUL. From the writings of CHARLES KINGSLEY. Extra fcap. 8vo. 3s. 6d.

DAILY THOUGHTS. Selected from the Writings of CHARLES KINGSLEY. By his Wife. Crown 8vo. 6s.

FROM DEATH TO LIFE. Fragments of Teaching to a Village Congregation. With Letters on the "Life after Death." Edited by his Wife. Fcap. 8vo. 2s. 6d.

Maclear (Rev. Canon).—A MANUAL OF INSTRUCTION FOR CONFIRMATION AND FIRST COMMUNION, WITH PRAYERS AND DEVOTIONS. 32mo. 2s.

THE HOUR OF SORROW; OR, THE OFFICE FOR THE BURIAL OF THE DEAD. 32mo. 2s.

Maurice (Frederick Denison).—LESSONS OF HOPE. Readings from the Works of F. D. MAURICE. Selected by Rev. J. Ll. DAVIES, M.A. Crown 8vo. 5s.

RAYS OF SUNLIGHT FOR DARK DAYS. With a Preface by Very Rev. C. J. VAUGHAN, D.D. New Edition. 18mo. 3s. 6d.

Service (Rev. John).—PRAYERS FOR PUBLIC WORSHIP. Crown 8vo. 4s. 6d.

THE WORSHIP OF GOD, AND FELLOWSHIP AMONG MEN. By FREDERICK DENISON MAURICE and others. Fcap. 8vo. 3s. 6d.

Welby-Gregory (The Hon. Lady).—LINKS AND CLUES. 2nd Edition. Crown 8vo. 6s.

Westcott (Rt. Rev. B. F., Bishop of Durham).—THOUGHTS ON REVELATION AND LIFE. Selections from the Writings of Bishop WESTCOTT. Edited by Rev. S. PHILLIPS. Crown 8vo. 6s.

Wilbraham (Frances M.)—IN THE SERE AND YELLOW LEAF: THOUGHTS AND RECOLLECTIONS FOR OLD AND YOUNG. Globe 8vo. 3s. 6d.

The Fathers

Cunningham (Rev. W.)—THE EPISTLE OF ST. BARNABAS. A Dissertation, including a Discussion of its Date and Authorship. Together with the Greek Text, the Latin Version, and a New English Translation and Commentary. Crown 8vo. 7s. 6d.

THEOLOGICAL CATALOGUE

Donaldson (Prof. James).—THE APOSTOLICAL FATHERS. A Critical Account of their Genuine Writings, and of their Doctrines. 2nd Edition. Crown 8vo. 7s. 6d.

Lightfoot (Bishop).—THE APOSTOLIC FATHERS. Part I. ST. CLEMENT OF ROME. Revised Texts, with Introductions, Notes, Dissertations, and Translations. 2 vols. 8vo. 32s.

THE APOSTOLIC FATHERS. Part II. ST. IGNATIUS to ST. POLYCARP. Revised Texts, with Introductions, Notes, Dissertations, and Translations. 3 vols. 2nd Edition. Demy 8vo. 48s.

THE APOSTOLIC FATHERS. Abridged Edition. With Short Introductions, Greek Text, and English Translation. 8vo. 16s.

Hymnology

Brooke (S. A.)—CHRISTIAN HYMNS. Edited and arranged. Fcap. 8vo. 2s. net.
This may also be had bound up with the Form of Service at Bedford Chapel, Bloomsbury. Price complete, 3s. net.

Palgrave (Prof. F. T.)—ORIGINAL HYMNS. 18mo. 1s. 6d.

Selborne (Roundell, Earl of)—
THE BOOK OF PRAISE. From the best English Hymn Writers. 18mo. 2s. 6d. net.
A HYMNAL. Chiefly from *The Book of Praise*. In various sizes. —A. Royal 32mo. 6d.—B. Small 18mo, larger type. 1s.—C. Same Edition, fine paper. 1s. 6d.—An Edition with Music, Selected, Harmonised, and Composed by JOHN HULLAH. Square 18mo. 3s. 6d.

Woods (M. A.)—HYMNS FOR SCHOOL WORSHIP. Compiled by M. A. WOODS. 18mo. 1s. 6d.

Sermons, Lectures, Addresses, and Theological Essays

(See also 'Bible,' 'Church of England,' 'Fathers.')

Abbot (Francis)—
SCIENTIFIC THEISM. Crown 8vo. 7s. 6d.
THE WAY OUT OF AGNOSTICISM: or, The Philosophy of Free Religion. Crown 8vo. 4s. 6d.

Abbott (Rev. E. A.)—
CAMBRIDGE SERMONS. 8vo. 6s.
OXFORD SERMONS. 8vo. 7s. 6d.
PHILOMYTHUS. An Antidote against Credulity. A discussion of Cardinal Newman's Essay on Ecclesiastical Miracles. 2nd Edition. Crown 8vo. 3s. 6d.
NEWMANIANISM. A Reply. Crown 8vo. Sewed, 1s. net.

Ainger (Rev. Alfred, Canon of Bristol).—SERMONS PREACHED IN THE TEMPLE CHURCH. Extra fcap. 8vo. 6s.

Alexander (W., Bishop of Derry and Raphoe).—THE LEADING IDEAS OF THE GOSPELS. New Edition, Revised and Enlarged. Crown 8vo. 6s.

Baines (Rev. Edward).—SERMONS. With a Preface and Memoir, by A. BARRY, D.D., late Bishop of Sydney. Crown 8vo. 6s.

Bather (Archdeacon).—ON SOME MINISTERIAL DUTIES, CATECHISING, PREACHING, ETC. Edited, with a Preface, by Very Rev. C. J. VAUGHAN, D.D. Fcap. 8vo. 4s. 6d.

Binnie (Rev. William).—SERMONS. Crown 8vo. 6s.

Birks (Thomas Rawson)—
  THE DIFFICULTIES OF BELIEF IN CONNECTION WITH THE CREATION AND THE FALL, REDEMPTION, AND JUDGMENT. 2nd Edition. Crown 8vo. 5s.
  JUSTIFICATION AND IMPUTED RIGHTEOUSNESS. Being a Review of Ten Sermons on the Nature and Effects of Faith, by JAMES THOMAS O'BRIEN, D.D., late Bishop of Ossory, Ferns, and Leighlin. Crown 8vo. 6s.
  SUPERNATURAL REVELATION : or, First Principles of Moral Theology. 8vo. 8s.

Brooke (Rev. Stopford A.)—SHORT SERMONS. Cr. 8vo. 6s.

Brooks (Phillips, Bishop of Massachusetts)—
  THE CANDLE OF THE LORD, and other Sermons. Crown 8vo. 6s.
  SERMONS PREACHED IN ENGLISH CHURCHES. Crown 8vo. 6s.
  TWENTY SERMONS. Crown 8vo. 6s.
  TOLERANCE. Crown 8vo. 2s. 6d.
  THE LIGHT OF THE WORLD. Crown 8vo. 3s. 6d.

Brunton (T. Lauder). — THE BIBLE AND SCIENCE. With Illustrations. Crown 8vo. 10s. 6d.

Butler (Rev. George).—SERMONS PREACHED IN CHELTENHAM COLLEGE CHAPEL. 8vo. 7s. 6d.

Butler (W. Archer)—
  SERMONS, DOCTRINAL AND PRACTICAL. 11th Edition. 8vo. 8s.
  SECOND SERIES OF SERMONS. 8vo. 7s.

Campbell (Dr. John M'Leod)—
  THE NATURE OF THE ATONEMENT. 6th Ed. Cr. 8vo. 6s.
  REMINISCENCES AND REFLECTIONS. Edited with an Introductory Narrative, by his Son, DONALD CAMPBELL, M.A. Crown 8vo. 7s. 6d.
  THOUGHTS ON REVELATION. 2nd Edition. Crown 8vo. 5s.
  RESPONSIBILITY FOR THE GIFT OF ETERNAL LIFE. Compiled from Sermons preached at Row, in the years 1829-31. Crown 8vo. 5s.

Canterbury (Edward White, Archbishop of)—
  BOY-LIFE : its Trial, its Strength, its Fulness. Sundays in Wellington College, 1859-73. 4th Edition. Crown 8vo. 6s.
  THE SEVEN GIFTS. Addressed to the Diocese of Canterbury in his Primary Visitation. 2nd Edition. Crown 8vo. 6s.
  CHRIST AND HIS TIMES. Addressed to the Diocese of Canterbury in his Second Visitation. Crown 8vo. 6s.

Carpenter (W. Boyd, Bishop of Ripon)—
  TRUTH IN TALE. Addresses, chiefly to Children. Crown 8vo. 4s. 6d.
  THE PERMANENT ELEMENTS OF RELIGION : Bampton Lectures, 1887. 2nd Edition. Crown 8vo. 6s.

Cazenove (J. Gibson).—CONCERNING THE BEING AND ATTRIBUTES OF GOD. 8vo. 5s.

Church (Dean)—
  HUMAN LIFE AND ITS CONDITIONS. Crown 8vo. 6s.
  THE GIFTS OF CIVILISATION, and other Sermons and Lectures. 2nd Edition. Crown 8vo. 7s. 6d.
  DISCIPLINE OF THE CHRISTIAN CHARACTER, and other Sermons. Crown 8vo. 4s. 6d.
  ADVENT SERMONS. 1885. Crown 8vo. 4s. 6d.
  VILLAGE SERMONS. Crown 8vo. 6s.
  CATHEDRAL AND UNIVERSITY SERMONS. Crown 8vo. 6s.
  CLERGYMAN'S SELF-EXAMINATION CONCERNING THE APOSTLES' CREED. Extra fcap. 8vo. 1s. 6d.

Congreve (Rev. John).—HIGH HOPES AND PLEADINGS FOR A REASONABLE FAITH, NOBLER THOUGHTS, LARGER CHARITY. Crown 8vo. 5s.

Cooke (Josiah P., Jun.)—RELIGION AND CHEMISTRY. Crown 8vo. 7s. 6d.

Cotton (Bishop).—SERMONS PREACHED TO ENGLISH CONGREGATIONS IN INDIA. Crown 8vo. 7s. 6d.

Cunningham (Rev. W.)—CHRISTIAN CIVILISATION, WITH SPECIAL REFERENCE TO INDIA. Cr. 8vo. 5s.

Curteis (Rev. G. H.)—THE SCIENTIFIC OBSTACLES TO CHRISTIAN BELIEF. The Boyle Lectures, 1884. Cr. 8vo. 6s.

Davies (Rev. J. Llewelyn)—
  THE GOSPEL AND MODERN LIFE. 2nd Edition, to which is added Morality according to the Sacrament of the Lord's Supper. Extra fcap. 8vo. 6s.
  SOCIAL QUESTIONS FROM THE POINT OF VIEW OF CHRISTIAN THEOLOGY. 2nd Edition. Crown 8vo. 6s.
  WARNINGS AGAINST SUPERSTITION. Extra fcap. 8vo. 2s. 6d.
  THE CHRISTIAN CALLING. Extra fcap. 8vo. 6s.
  ORDER AND GROWTH AS INVOLVED IN THE SPIRITUAL CONSTITUTION OF HUMAN SOCIETY. Crown 8vo. 3s. 6d.

Davies (Rev. J. Llewelyn)—*continued.*
BAPTISM, CONFIRMATION, AND THE LORD'S SUPPER, as interpreted by their Outward Signs. Three Addresses. New Edition. 18mo. 1s.

Diggle (Rev. J. W.)—GODLINESS AND MANLINESS. A Miscellany of Brief Papers touching the Relation of Religion to Life. Crown 8vo. 6s.

Drummond (Prof. James).—INTRODUCTION TO THE STUDY OF THEOLOGY. Crown 8vo. 5s.

ECCE HOMO. A Survey of the Life and Work of Jesus Christ. 20th Edition. Globe 8vo. 6s.

Ellerton (Rev. John).—THE HOLIEST MANHOOD, AND ITS LESSONS FOR BUSY LIVES. Crown 8vo. 6s.

FAITH AND CONDUCT: An Essay on Verifiable Religion. Crown 8vo. 7s. 6d.

Farrar (Ven. F. W., Archdeacon of Westminster)—
THE HISTORY OF INTERPRETATION. Being the Bampton Lectures, 1885. 8vo. 16s.

Collected Edition of the Sermons, etc. Crown 8vo. 3s. 6d. each.
SEEKERS AFTER GOD.
ETERNAL HOPE. Sermons Preached in Westminster Abbey.
THE FALL OF MAN, and other Sermons.
THE WITNESS OF HISTORY TO CHRIST. Hulsean Lectures.
THE SILENCE AND VOICES OF GOD.
IN THE DAYS OF THY YOUTH. Sermons on Practical Subjects.
SAINTLY WORKERS. Five Lenten Lectures.
EPHPHATHA: or, The Amelioration of the World.
MERCY AND JUDGMENT. A few last words on Christian Eschatology.
SERMONS AND ADDRESSES delivered in America.

Fiske (John).—MAN'S DESTINY VIEWED IN THE LIGHT OF HIS ORIGIN. Crown 8vo. 3s. 6d.

Forbes (Rev. Granville).—THE VOICE OF GOD IN THE PSALMS. Crown 8vo. 6s. 6d.

Fowle (Rev. T. W.)—A NEW ANALOGY BETWEEN REVEALED RELIGION AND THE COURSE AND CONSTITUTION OF NATURE. Crown 8vo. 6s.

Fraser (Bishop).—SERMONS. Edited by Rev. JOHN W. DIGGLE. 2 vols. Crown 8vo. 6s. each.

Hamilton (John)—
ON TRUTH AND ERROR. Crown 8vo. 5s.
ARTHUR'S SEAT: or, The Church of the Banned. Crown 8vo. 6s.
ABOVE AND AROUND: Thoughts on God and Man. 12mo. 2s. 6d.

Hardwick (Archdeacon).—CHRIST AND OTHER MASTERS. 6th Edition. Crown 8vo. 10s. 6d.

Hare (Julius Charles)—
  THE MISSION OF THE COMFORTER. New Edition. Edited by Dean PLUMPTRE. Crown 8vo. 7s. 6d.
  THE VICTORY OF FAITH. Edited by Dean PLUMPTRE, with Introductory Notices by Prof. MAURICE and Dean STANLEY. Crown 8vo. 6s. 6d.
Harper (Father Thomas, S.J.)—THE METAPHYSICS OF THE SCHOOL. In 5 vols. Vols. I. and II. 8vo. 18s. each. Vol. III. Part I. 12s.
Harris (Rev. G. C.) — SERMONS. With a Memoir by CHARLOTTE M. YONGE, and Portrait. Extra fcap. 8vo. 6s.
Hutton (R. H.)—
  ESSAYS ON SOME OF THE MODERN GUIDES OF ENGLISH THOUGHT IN MATTERS OF FAITH. Globe 8vo. 6s.
  THEOLOGICAL ESSAYS. Globe 8vo. 6s.
Illingworth (Rev. J. R.)—SERMONS PREACHED IN A COLLEGE CHAPEL. Crown 8vo. 5s.
  UNIVERSITY AND CATHEDRAL SERMONS. Crown 8vo. [*In the Press.*]
Jacob (Rev. J. A.) — BUILDING IN SILENCE, and other Sermons. Extra fcap. 8vo. 6s.
James (Rev. Herbert).—THE COUNTRY CLERGYMAN AND HIS WORK. Crown 8vo. 6s.
Jeans (Rev. G. E.)—HAILEYBURY CHAPEL, and other Sermons. Fcap. 8vo. 3s. 6d.
Jellett (Rev. Dr.)—
  THE ELDER SON, and other Sermons. Crown 8vo. 6s.
  THE EFFICACY OF PRAYER. 3rd Edition. Crown 8vo. 5s.
Kellogg (Rev. S. H.)—THE LIGHT OF ASIA AND THE LIGHT OF THE WORLD. Crown 8vo. 7s. 6d.
  THE GENESIS AND GROWTH OF RELIGION. Cr. 8vo. 6s.
Kingsley (Charles)—
  VILLAGE AND TOWN AND COUNTRY SERMONS. Crown 8vo. 3s. 6d.
  THE WATER OF LIFE, and other Sermons. Crown 8vo. 3s. 6d.
  SERMONS ON NATIONAL SUBJECTS, AND THE KING OF THE EARTH. Crown 8vo. 3s. 6d.
  SERMONS FOR THE TIMES. Crown 8vo. 3s. 6d.
  GOOD NEWS OF GOD. Crown 8vo. 3s. 6d.
  THE GOSPEL OF THE PENTATEUCH, AND DAVID. Crown 8vo. 3s. 6d.
  DISCIPLINE, and other Sermons. Crown 8vo. 3s. 6d.
  WESTMINSTER SERMONS. Crown 8vo. 3s. 6d.
  ALL SAINTS' DAY, and other Sermons. Crown 8vo. 3s. 6d.
Kirkpatrick (Prof. A. F.)—THE DIVINE LIBRARY OF THE OLD TESTAMENT. Its Origin, Preservation, Inspiration, and Permanent Value. Crown 8vo. 3s. net.

Kirkpatrick (Prof. A. F.)—*continued.*
  THE DOCTRINE OF THE PROPHETS. Warburtonian Lectures 1886-1890. Crown 8vo. 6s.

Kynaston (Rev. Herbert, D.D.)—SERMONS PREACHED IN THE COLLEGE CHAPEL, CHELTENHAM. Crown 8vo. 6s.

Lightfoot (Bishop)—
  LEADERS IN THE NORTHERN CHURCH : Sermons Preached in the Diocese of Durham. 2nd Edition. Crown 8vo. 6s.
  ORDINATION ADDRESSES AND COUNSELS TO CLERGY. Crown 8vo. 6s.
  CAMBRIDGE SERMONS. Crown 8vo. 6s.
  SERMONS PREACHED IN ST. PAUL'S CATHEDRAL. Crown 8vo. 6s.
  SERMONS PREACHED ON SPECIAL OCCASIONS. Crown 8vo. 6s.
  A CHARGE DELIVERED TO THE CLERGY OF THE DIOCESE OF DURHAM, 25th Nov. 1886. Demy 8vo. 2s.
  ESSAYS ON THE WORK ENTITLED "Supernatural Religion." 8vo. 10s. 6d.
  DISSERTATIONS ON THE APOSTOLIC AGE. 8vo. 14s.
  BIBLICAL MISCELLANIES. 8vo. [*In the Press.*

Maclaren (Rev. Alexander)—
  SERMONS PREACHED AT MANCHESTER. 11th Edition. Fcap. 8vo. 4s. 6d.
  A SECOND SERIES OF SERMONS. 7th Ed. Fcap. 8vo. 4s. 6d.
  A THIRD SERIES. 6th Edition. Fcap. 8vo. 4s. 6d.
  WEEK-DAY EVENING ADDRESSES. 4th Ed. Fcap. 8vo. 2s. 6d.
  THE SECRET OF POWER, AND OTHER SERMONS. Fcap. 8vo. 4s. 6d.

Macmillan (Rev. Hugh)—
  BIBLE TEACHINGS IN NATURE. 15th Ed. Globe 8vo. 6s.
  THE TRUE VINE ; OR, THE ANALOGIES OF OUR LORD'S ALLEGORY. 5th Edition. Globe 8vo. 6s.
  THE MINISTRY OF NATURE. 8th Edition. Globe 8vo. 6s.
  THE SABBATH OF THE FIELDS. 6th Edition. Globe 8vo. 6s.
  THE MARRIAGE IN CANA. Globe 8vo. 6s.
  TWO WORLDS ARE OURS. 3rd Edition. Globe 8vo. 6s.
  THE OLIVE LEAF. Globe 8vo. 6s.
  THE GATE BEAUTIFUL AND OTHER BIBLE TEACHINGS FOR THE YOUNG. Crown 8vo. 3s. 6d.

Mahaffy (Rev. Prof.)—THE DECAY OF MODERN PREACHING : AN ESSAY. Crown 8vo. 3s. 6d.

Maturin (Rev. W.)—THE BLESSEDNESS OF THE DEAD IN CHRIST. Crown 8vo. 7s. 6d.

Maurice (Frederick Denison)—
  THE KINGDOM OF CHRIST. 3rd Ed. 2 Vols. Cr. 8vo. 12s.
  EXPOSITORY SERMONS ON THE PRAYER-BOOK ; AND ON THE LORD'S PRAYER. New Edition. Crown 8vo. 6s.

Maurice (Frederick Denison)—*continued.*
SERMONS PREACHED IN COUNTRY CHURCHES. 2nd Edition. Crown 8vo. 6s.
THE CONSCIENCE. Lectures on Casuistry. 3rd Ed. Cr. 8vo. 4s. 6d.
DIALOGUES ON FAMILY WORSHIP. Crown 8vo. 4s. 6d.
THE DOCTRINE OF SACRIFICE DEDUCED FROM THE SCRIPTURES. 2nd Edition. Crown 8vo. 6s.
THE RELIGIONS OF THE WORLD. 6th Edition. Cr. 8vo. 4s. 6d.
ON THE SABBATH DAY; THE CHARACTER OF THE WARRIOR; AND ON THE INTERPRETATION OF HISTORY. Fcap. 8vo. 2s. 6d.
LEARNING AND WORKING. Crown 8vo. 4s. 6d.
THE LORD'S PRAYER, THE CREED, AND THE COMMANDMENTS. 18mo. 1s.
SERMONS PREACHED IN LINCOLN'S INN CHAPEL. In Six Volumes. Crown 8vo. 3s. 6d. each.

Collected Works. Monthly Volumes from October 1892. Crown 8vo. 3s. 6d. each.
CHRISTMAS DAY AND OTHER SERMONS.
THEOLOGICAL ESSAYS.
PROPHETS AND KINGS.
PATRIARCHS AND LAWGIVERS.
THE GOSPEL OF THE KINGDOM OF HEAVEN.
GOSPEL OF ST. JOHN.
EPISTLE OF ST. JOHN.
LECTURES ON THE APOCALYPSE.
FRIENDSHIP OF BOOKS.
SOCIAL MORALITY.
PRAYER BOOK AND LORD'S PRAYER.
THE DOCTRINE OF SACRIFICE.

Milligan (Rev. Prof. W.)—THE RESURRECTION OF OUR LORD. Fourth Thousand. Crown 8vo. 5s.
THE ASCENSION AND HEAVENLY PRIESTHOOD OF OUR LORD. *Baird Lectures*, 1891. Crown 8vo. 7s. 6d.

Moorhouse (J., Bishop of Manchester)—
JACOB: Three Sermons. Extra fcap. 8vo. 3s. 6d.
THE TEACHING OF CHRIST. Its Conditions, Secret, and Results. Crown 8vo. 3s. net.

Mylne (L. G., Bishop of Bombay).—SERMONS PREACHED IN ST. THOMAS'S CATHEDRAL, BOMBAY. Crown 8vo. 6s.
NATURAL RELIGION. By the author of "Ecce Homo." 3rd Edition. Globe 8vo. 6s.

Pattison (Mark).—SERMONS. Crown 8vo. 6s.
PAUL OF TARSUS. 8vo. 10s. 6d.
PHILOCHRISTUS. Memoirs of a Disciple of the Lord. 3rd Ed. 8vo. 12s.

Plumptre (Dean). — MOVEMENTS IN RELIGIOUS THOUGHT. Fcap. 8vo. 3s. 6d.

Potter (R.)—THE RELATION OF ETHICS TO RELIGION. Crown 8vo. 2s. 6d.

REASONABLE FAITH: A Short Religious Essay for the Times. By "Three Friends." Crown 8vo. 1s.

Reichel (C. P., Bishop of Meath)—
THE LORD'S PRAYER, and other Sermons. Crown 8vo. 7s. 6d.
CATHEDRAL AND UNIVERSITY SERMONS. Crown 8vo. 6s.

Rendall (Rev. F.)—THE THEOLOGY OF THE HEBREW CHRISTIANS. Crown 8vo. 5s.

Reynolds (H. R.)—NOTES OF THE CHRISTIAN LIFE. Crown 8vo. 7s. 6d.

Robinson (Prebendary H. G.)—MAN IN THE IMAGE OF GOD, and other Sermons. Crown 8vo. 7s. 6d.

Russell (Dean).—THE LIGHT THAT LIGHTETH EVERY MAN : Sermons. With an introduction by Dean PLUMPTRE, D.D. Crown 8vo. 6s.

Salmon (Rev. Prof. George)—
NON-MIRACULOUS CHRISTIANITY, and other Sermons. 2nd Edition. Crown 8vo. 6s.
GNOSTICISM AND AGNOSTICISM, and other Sermons. Crown 8vo. 7s. 6d.

Sandford (C. W., Bishop of Gibraltar).—COUNSEL TO ENGLISH CHURCHMEN ABROAD. Crown 8vo. 6s.

SCOTCH SERMONS, 1880. By Principal CAIRD and others. 3rd Edition. 8vo. 10s. 6d.

Service (Rev. John).—SERMONS. With Portrait. Crown 8vo. 6s.

Shirley (W. N.)—ELIJAH : Four University Sermons. Fcap. 8vo. 2s. 6d.

Smith (Rev. Travers).—MAN'S KNOWLEDGE OF MAN AND OF GOD. Crown 8vo. 6s.

Smith (W. Saumarez).—THE BLOOD OF THE NEW COVENANT : A Theological Essay. Crown 8vo. 2s. 6d.

Stanley (Dean)—
THE NATIONAL THANKSGIVING. Sermons preached in Westminster Abbey. 2nd Edition. Crown 8vo. 2s. 6d.
ADDRESSES AND SERMONS delivered during a visit to the United States and Canada in 1878. Crown 8vo. 6s.

Stewart (Prof. Balfour) and **Tait** (Prof. P. G.)—THE UNSEEN UNIVERSE; OR, PHYSICAL SPECULATIONS ON A FUTURE STATE. 15th Edition. Crown 8vo. 6s.
PARADOXICAL PHILOSOPHY : A Sequel to "The Unseen Universe." Crown 8vo. 7s. 6d.

Stubbs (Rev. C. W.)—FOR CHRIST AND CITY. Sermons and Addresses. Crown 8vo. 6s.

Tait (Archbishop)—
THE PRESENT POSITION OF THE CHURCH OF ENGLAND.
Being the Charge delivered at his Primary Visitation. 8vo. 3s. 6d.
DUTIES OF THE CHURCH OF ENGLAND. Being seven
Addresses delivered at his Second Visitation. 8vo. 4s. 6d.
THE CHURCH OF THE FUTURE. Charges delivered at his
Third Quadrennial Visitation. 2nd Edition. Crown 8vo. 3s. 6d.

Taylor (Isaac).—THE RESTORATION OF BELIEF. Crown
8vo. 8s. 6d.

Temple (Frederick, Bishop of London)—
SERMONS PREACHED IN THE CHAPEL OF RUGBY
SCHOOL. SECOND SERIES. 3rd Edition. Extra fcap. 8vo. 6s.
THIRD SERIES. 4th Edition. Extra fcap. 8vo. 6s.
THE RELATIONS BETWEEN RELIGION AND SCIENCE.
Bampton Lectures, 1884. 7th and Cheaper Ed. Cr. 8vo. 6s.

Trench (Archbishop).—HULSEAN LECTURES. 8vo. 7s. 6d.

Tulloch (Principal).—THE CHRIST OF THE GOSPELS
AND THE CHRIST OF MODERN CRITICISM. Extra
fcap. 8vo. 4s. 6d.

Vaughan (C. J., Dean of Llandaff)—
MEMORIALS OF HARROW SUNDAYS. 5th Edition. Crown
8vo. 10s. 6d.
EPIPHANY, LENT, AND EASTER. 3rd Ed. Cr. 8vo. 10s. 6d.
HEROES OF FAITH. 2nd Edition. Crown 8vo. 6s.
LIFE'S WORK AND GOD'S DISCIPLINE. 3rd Edition.
Extra fcap. 8vo. 2s. 6d.
THE WHOLESOME WORDS OF JESUS CHRIST. 2nd
Edition. Fcap. 8vo. 3s. 6d.
FOES OF FAITH. 2nd Edition. Fcap. 8vo. 3s. 6d.
CHRIST SATISFYING THE INSTINCTS OF HUMANITY.
2nd Edition. Extra fcap. 8vo. 3s. 6d.
COUNSELS FOR YOUNG STUDENTS. Fcap. 8vo. 2s. 6d.
THE TWO GREAT TEMPTATIONS. 2nd Ed. Fcap. 8vo. 3s. 6d.
ADDRESSES FOR YOUNG CLERGYMEN. Extra fcap. 8vo.
4s. 6d.
"MY SON, GIVE ME THINE HEART." Extra fcap. 8vo. 5s.
REST AWHILE. Addresses to Toilers in the Ministry. Extra fcap.
8vo. 5s.
TEMPLE SERMONS. Crown 8vo. 10s. 6d.
AUTHORISED OR REVISED? Sermons on some of the Texts in
which the Revised Version differs from the Authorised. Crown
8vo. 7s. 6d.
LESSONS OF THE CROSS AND PASSION. WORDS FROM
THE CROSS. THE REIGN OF SIN. THE LORD'S
PRAYER. Four Courses of Lent Lectures. Crown 8vo. 10s. 6d.
UNIVERSITY SERMONS. NEW AND OLD. Cr. 8vo. 10s. 6d.

Vaughan (C. J., Dean of Llandaff)—*continued.*
  NOTES FOR LECTURES ON CONFIRMATION. Fcap. 8vo. 1s. 6d.
  THE PRAYERS OF JESUS CHRIST: a closing volume of Lent Lectures delivered in the Temple Church. Globe 8vo. 3s. 6d.
  DONCASTER SERMONS. Lessons of Life and Godliness, and Words from the Gospels. Cr. 8vo. 10s. 6d.
  RESTFUL THOUGHTS IN RESTLESS TIMES. Crown 8vo. [*In the Press.*

Vaughan (Rev. D. J.)—THE PRESENT TRIAL OF FAITH. Crown 8vo. 9s.

Vaughan (Rev. E. T.)—SOME REASONS OF OUR CHRISTIAN HOPE. Hulsean Lectures for 1875. Crown 8vo. 6s. 6d.

Vaughan (Rev. Robert).—STONES FROM THE QUARRY. Sermons. Crown 8vo. 5s.

Venn (Rev. John).—ON SOME CHARACTERISTICS OF BELIEF, SCIENTIFIC AND RELIGIOUS. 8vo. 6s. 6d.

Warington (G.)—THE WEEK OF CREATION. Cr. 8vo. 4s. 6d.

Welldon (Rev. J. E. C.)—THE SPIRITUAL LIFE, and other Sermons. Crown 8vo. 6s.

Westcott (B. F., Bishop of Durham)—
  ON THE RELIGIOUS OFFICE OF THE UNIVERSITIES. Sermons. Crown 8vo. 4s. 6d.
  GIFTS FOR MINISTRY. Addresses to Candidates for Ordination. Crown 8vo. 1s. 6d.
  THE VICTORY OF THE CROSS. Sermons preached during Holy Week, 1888, in Hereford Cathedral. Crown 8vo. 3s. 6d.
  FROM STRENGTH TO STRENGTH. Three Sermons (In Memoriam J. B. D.) Crown 8vo. 2s.
  THE REVELATION OF THE RISEN LORD. Cr. 8vo. 6s.
  THE HISTORIC FAITH. 3rd Edition. Crown 8vo. 6s.
  THE GOSPEL OF THE RESURRECTION. 6th Ed. Cr. 8vo. 6s.
  THE REVELATION OF THE FATHER. Crown 8vo. 6s.
  CHRISTUS CONSUMMATOR. 2nd Edition. Crown 8vo. 6s.
  SOME THOUGHTS FROM THE ORDINAL. Cr. 8vo. 1s. 6d.
  SOCIAL ASPECTS OF CHRISTIANITY. Crown 8vo. 6s.
  ESSAYS IN THE HISTORY OF RELIGIOUS THOUGHT IN THE WEST. Globe 8vo. 6s.
  THE GOSPEL OF LIFE. Cr. 8vo. 6s.

Wickham (Rev. E. C.)—WELLINGTON COLLEGE SERMONS. Crown 8vo. 6s.

Wilkins (Prof. A. S.)—THE LIGHT OF THE WORLD: an Essay. 2nd Edition. Crown 8vo. 3s. 6d.

Wilson (J. M., Archdeacon of Manchester)—
  SERMONS PREACHED IN CLIFTON COLLEGE CHAPEL. Second Series. 1888-90. Crown 8vo. 6s.
  ESSAYS AND ADDRESSES. Crown 8vo. 4s. 6d.
  SOME CONTRIBUTIONS TO THE RELIGIOUS THOUGHT OF OUR TIME. Crown 8vo. 6s.

Printed by R. & R. CLARK, *Edinburgh*

www.ingramcontent.com/pod-product-compliance
Lightning Source LLC
Chambersburg PA
CBHW021728220426
43662CB00008B/751